OLD SHIP PRINTS

(Page 29)

THE CITY OF TREVISO WITH A CARRACK.
From "The Nuremberg Chronicle," 1493.

PLATE 1

Old Ship
PRINTS

BY
E. KEBLE CHATTERTON

SPRING BOOKS · LONDON

First published in 1927
by John Lane The Bodley Head Limited. Copyright

This edition published 1965 *by Spring Books*
Drury House, Russell Street, London WC2
Second Impression 1967

Printed in Great Britain
by Richard Clay (The Chaucer Press) Ltd., Bungay, Suffolk

PREFACE

THE title of this volume is sufficiently indicative of its scope. Herein will be found prints of every kind of sailing ship which the engravers in the past sought to illustrate. Galleys, carracks, merchantmen and men-of-war, clippers, fore-and-afters, yachts, are all presented as they appeared to contemporary masters. At the same time we are afforded invaluable details concerning the voyages, the seafaring and the nautical life generally during the centuries. So many letters asking for such details continue to reach me from different countries that it is hoped a study of these carefully selected prints may be of assistance.

The latter are meant to be regarded not as making up a mere picture-book, but as references for those who wish to appreciate the marine side of history and to visualize the conditions of byegone explorers, traders, fighters, and so on. The quiet pondering over these prints with the magnifying glass will reveal many an interesting point concerning the ships themselves and the manner of their handling. How, indeed, can we read, with understanding, Hakluyt or any other collection of old sailing-ship voyages, unless we can have before us some accurate and detailed idea of the vessels according to their categories? It is my hope, therefore, that these pages may interest not merely the print connoisseur; the artists seeking reliable information for their sea pictures; the makers of ship models; but also the general reader who desires to reconstruct the past.

I have to acknowledge my indebtedness to Mr. A. G. H. Macpherson for permission to use items from his remarkable collection. The following authorities have been consulted in the course of this volume: Bryan's "Dictionary of Painters and Engravers," Slater's "Engravings and Their Values," Willshire's "Introduction to the Study and Collection of Ancient Prints," Jackson and Chatto's "Treatise on Wood Engraving," Woodbury's "History of Wood Engraving," Dr. F. Lippmann's "Art of Wood Engraving in Italy," H. W. Davies' monograph on "Bernhard von Breydenbach," Hind's "Guide to the Processes and Schools of Engraving," Sir Sidney Colvin's "Early Engraving and Engravers in England," and Bénézet's "Dictionnaire Critique et documentaire des Peintres, Sculpteurs, Dessinateurs et Graveurs."

For the rest I have relied on my own independent researches covering a period of many years.   E. KEBLE CHATTERTON.

PUBLISHER'S NOTE TO 1965 EDITION

Mr. E. Keble Chatterton's book was originally published in 1927 and this edition differs from the earlier one only in a minor readjustment of the sequence of pictures and in the necessity of reproducing several coloured illustrations in black-and-white, owing to the destruction of the original blocks. The text is unchanged, save for a few altered references arising from the pictorial rearrangement. It seems hardly necessary, therefore, to point out that some of the author's references to availability of prints, to dealers and collections, and, alas, to purchase prices, are inapplicable to the present day. Happily, many of the prints are still in circulation, so that, despite changing values, the author's discriminating judgment and taste can still serve as a reliable guide for the modern collector.

The author also refers several times to a special edition of his book. This was limited to 100 copies and is, of course, unobtainable today.

CONTENTS

LIST OF ILLUSTRATIONS

COLOUR

IN THE TEXT

OLD SHIP PRINTS

CHAPTER I

INTRODUCTION

It is the nature of man to surround himself by those things which he loves, and he exhibits his tastes with the greatest emphasis by the character of his immediate environment. To an imaginative mind the collecting of any reproduced picture is an instinct dating back right to infancy, developed in youth and modified by knowledge. A child finds delight in the printed design, the schoolboy proceeds to assemble in a scrapbook his favourite representations, the adult selects and discards and acquires for his portfolio : it is the same acquisitive impulse running through the seven ages of man, handed down from generation to posterity.

It is noticeable that, quite apart from any appeal to the emotions by line or colour, the human being finds an unrivalled pleasure in the representation of people and things, even when these are of the most familiar character. Hence, in the broadest sense, portraits and landscapes will always have a wonderful appeal, for the reason that they are understood by the universal mind. But in an entirely special and selected circle, which is interested by all that is summed up in the romance of seafaring, there is an even more powerful fascination when maritime activity is shown concentrated in one single work of art. Enthusiasm here reaches wonderful heights, the æsthetic pleasure obtained is beyond all limits. As evidence of this, you have only to show an old shellback an accurate model or picture of a sailing-ship and see how his china-blue eyes instantly light up. All his life has been spent in or about such a vessel; and yet the reproduction of that very thing creates in him spontaneous joy.

Thus, in the same way, a large public which loves beautiful things and feels an attraction towards salt water derives a peculiar enjoyment in gathering some imagery that will conjure up again those sensations which have been incited on some occasion by the sight of a ship under sail on a sunlit sea. The boy who used to surround himself with cheap photographs or cigarette-cards now, as a grown-up amateur of art, collects valuable sea-paintings if he has the means and house room; or, failing that condition, he sets out to obtain at moderate costs the best nautical prints that diligent search, restricted supply, and an increasing demand will allow. It is possible by means of these prints to gain an accurate and pictorial history of seafaring during the most important four centuries. No period in maritime progress has seen such vital development as that from the latter part of the fifteenth century to the end of the nineteenth, covering as it does the growth of the ship from a mere coaster to a fast ocean-going craft fit to go all over the seven seas, and fit to lie in line-of-battle with a hundred guns; but finally to be eclipsed by the wonders of steel and steam.

During the last few years two factors have contributed to creating an unprecedented concern in these ship prints. Just as one never fully appreciates a treasure until it is taken away from one, so it was not till the sailing ship had almost disappeared from the ocean highway that people began to realize the romantic pedigree which she possessed. They insisted on knowing all about her, how she evolved, how the crews fared, what sort of passages were made, what the ships looked like. Thus the final expression of three-, four- and even five-masted sailing vessels became of great importance to a considerable section of our contemporaries. But, secondly, there was the influence of the war. Both in Europe and America the possibilities of naval operations in regard to raw materials and food supplies focused the public gaze on the sea. The sailing ship herself was, time after time, sent to the bottom by mine and torpedo and her place was taken by the steamer. Similarly there was begotten a new enthusiasm for the old naval prints depicting those long-drawn-out hostilities of the seventeenth, eighteenth, and early nineteenth centuries. And all this reawakening coincided with the changed bias in favour of old furniture, old architecture, old plate, old clocks, old tapestries and so on.

Thus, to-day, there are probably more collectors of old ship prints than ever, for, most unfortunately, photography was only just coming in as the sailing ship of the clipper period was going out. Therefore, if we wish to see an accurate picture of a frigate action, or an eighteenth-century East Indiaman, we have to rely either on a contemporary painting or print. Unquestionably the market price is rising, but it is still possible to find in some out-of-the-way place many a woodcut, aquatint, line engraving, or even lithograph whose value has been forgotten for years. Whilst there has recently occurred a veritable deluge of fake ship-models from Germany, which can have no possible value, a similar expenditure of money can obtain authentic old prints that can never depreciate but must become rarer as time goes on.

In this volume I have endeavoured to give the collector a comprehensive and representative series of nautical prints from the year 1486 to the year 1895. During this space of time we shall be able to trace the very earliest efforts of the engravers, down to the supreme productions of the lithographer, in their desire to show us what the ships of their period resembled. But herein will be found something more than the mere external appearance ; for by reference to these old maps and plans, lively representations of incidents at sea, intimate pictures of life on board, of exploration and discovery, naval actions, harbours and maritime views, shipyards, whaling, Revenue cutters, schooners, clippers, smacks, yachts, naval uniforms and caricatures, it is possible to visualize that which we have learned from documents. The facts take on an animation that enables us to be shipmates with the voyagers in their different shipping. Indeed, but for certain of these fifteenth- and sixteenth-century prints, our knowledge of seafaring at its springtime of achievement would be extremely scant. For, until the invention of printing there were scarcely any reproductions of maritime endeavour, if we omit such attempts as coins, seals, stained glass windows, sculpture—none of them too accurate.

It is true that occasionally the mediæval masters of painting depicted casually a ship or boat as part of the story. But there was no such thing as a school of maritime artists until, in the seventeenth century, the Dutch had learned the potentialities as well as the terrors of the sea. They began to paint ships and seapieces solely because they delighted in maritime things, and the Van der Veldes started the tradition in England. But before that period we have to rely on the work of the wood-cutter and line-engraver for those intimate and invaluable details that we yearn to know, and confirm the limited knowledge which we possess from the sources mentioned, in addition to such items as manuscripts and illuminated Hour-books. We are, therefore, very grateful to the early artists of prints. These early English and foreign examples are not always easy to obtain, but collections are frequently broken up after the death of their owner, so that, if one knows what to desire, the attainment of some special print is not so unlikely as might be supposed.

Prints vary so much in quality, their realizable value changes so considerably with the fashion of the moment, that inevitably prices must fluctuate. In buying one has to take into account whether the print has been retouched, whether it is badly printed, or weakly printed, or cut. It may have been published as a separate and individual unit, or again it may have been extracted from some printed book. These considerations have to be reckoned more closely by the collector who is purchasing with a view to investment, though to the keen ship-lover they are less weighty. In their educational value, as showing collaterally the development of engraving and shipping, a chronologically arranged series of prints even of inferior state and impression, definitely illustrating such themes as rigging, sail-plans, naval architecture, the story of sea-power, or some particular period such as the Anglo-French wars, cannot fail to be worth all the money one may feel able to expend on this hobby.

With this mental organization of taste the collector can proceed to look through the parcels of prints not merely at the few first-class printsellers', but at sales, in second-hand bookshops and among lumber heaps. It is for this reason that the following chapters may be found useful in showing the reader what is worth seeking and why. These instances have all been carefully selected from the famous Macpherson Collection, which is the finest in the world and is now valued at little short of £100,000. Built up in a comparatively short space of time from quite small beginnings, it shows what can be achieved by others sufficiently zealous of the subject. For the average person with that indescribable affection towards things nautical it is well to aim first at quality rather than quantity within the scope decided upon. A good example of " The Glorious First of June " may not be picked up the first day at the required price, but it is worth waiting for, especially if it is an aquatint in colour by such a master as Dodd. After a while it will be possible for the collector to discard, as his portfolio becomes fuller ; the ultimate objective being to cover a certain subject or period with the best examples, in the best states, by the best engravers.

To the English-speaking peoples ship prints have an especial appeal, for they are essentially the expression of faith in the sea and ocean travel. Those of the late sixteenth and seventeenth centuries are so full of the wonders found in remote corners of the world, that these illustrations are too set on dramatic exultation to worry much about consecutive incident. So very few people used the sea, and with their own eyes beheld the strange lands and natives, that the stay-at-homes must be roused pictorially. And when we come to the eighteenth century, with all its international and political crises, these scenes of battles and single-ship engagements are the emotional reaction to stirring times. The protected hailed their protectors ; English homes were decorated with prints showing the glorious deeds of their deliverers ; portraits of gallant and red-nosed admirals ; scenes showing roisterous seamen on leave after their hard service afloat ; fleets sailing in line ahead, ships limping home, heroes perishing melodramatically, spars crashing down amid the din and thunder of guns—all this gives us a far truer idea of the spirit that animated the age than we can learn from the cold calculated documents of the time. Just as a series of photographs taken in Piccadilly Circus at midday on November 11, 1918, will afford to posterity the exact effect of the Armistice on the citizens of London, so these contemporary prints impress us with the way they reflect our forefathers' attitude in time of triumph through suspense at sea.

Before proceeding further it may be convenient to define briefly the use of certain terms. Speaking generally, the art of engraving is that of cutting lines on wood or metal. Thus we have woodcuts, wood-engravings, engravings and etchings on metal. In the woodcuts and wood-engravings the parts of the design intended to print white are cut away by a knife or graver. The black lines are left in relief. The earliest impressions on paper from wood-blocks do not date until about the end of the fourteenth century, for the reason that sufficient paper was not procurable ; and it was in Germany as well as the Netherlands that most of the earliest woodcuts were produced. The earliest date engraved on a woodcut is 1423, but the earliest printed book with woodcuts appeared about 1460, and woodcut illustrations did not become usual in Germany until after another decade. Nor did it follow that the artist who made the designs always actually cut away the wood.

Engraving on metal, such as copper, iron, pewter or silver, followed that of wood-cutting for purposes of reproduction ; yet engraving on metal for the sole purpose of decoration is far older. As part of the goldsmith's art it went back to ancient times, it was continued through the Middle Ages, but not till the fifteenth century was it employed for printing a design on paper ; the earliest date on any line-engraving print being about 1446, though perhaps a decade before this line-engraving was being used for making playing cards. The greatest line-engraver in Germany at the full develop-ment of the art was, of course, Albrecht Dürer of Nuremberg, where he was apprenticed to Michael Wohlgemuth, Dürer's period covering the period 1471 to 1528. We shall mention Wohlgemuth again presently.

Etching is the process of eating into the plate by means of acid after the copper has been opened by means of a steel needle. This method was used by the fifteenth century armourers for decorating their iron ; but the earliest dated application of etching to reproduction is 1513, and Dürer himself etched a few plates. But woodcuts, line-engravings and etchings are all lacking in tone. It was the invention of mezzotint by Ludwig von Sigen (born in 1609) which employed the method of engraving by scraping the plate after it had been roughed all over ; and thus obtained a process which gave half tones. Introduced into England by Prince Rupert, it was used for engraving many of Sir Joshua Reynolds's finest paintings and portraits of contemporary admirals.

Similarly, stipple-engraving endeavours by dots or flicks to give tone to a plate, and here again there is a debt to the goldsmiths' engravers, though it was really Bartolozzi (1728—1813) who gave the vogue to this method. Aquatint, however, is the etching process which gives the nearest approach that prints can ever offer in regard to sepia drawings, the effect being obtained by biting the copper plate with the *aqua fortis*, or nitric acid. In this process not lines but areas are bitten, and the result is an imitation of the washes by water-colour. It was devised in the latter half of the eighteenth century by Jean Baptiste Le Prince. Finally came Aloys Senefelder (1771—1834), who invented the art of lithography by which a surface print can be taken from stone. It is by this means that so many illustrations of the famous vessels of the nineteenth century, in the full glory of their development, have survived for our admiration.

But, also, we must add as introduction to our study a few remarks on colour printing and its relation to the modern " fakes " and semi-" fakes " ; for it will greatly assist the uninterrupted progress of our story if these technical matters can be appreciated from the first.

The divisions of printing are three, and the employment of the above-mentioned blocks, or plates, or stones, is assigned as follows. First of all comes Relief Printing wherein there are used the wood-cut, the wood-engraving and the metal plates which have been etched, cut, or engraved *in relief*. This corresponds to the method of printing from type ; that is to say the impression is obtained from the parts which stand out after the incision has been performed. Secondly, we have the exact opposite of this and name it Intaglio Printing, for the paper receives the ink not from the outstanding relief but from the incised hollows which have been made in the metal plate ; and it is under this category that we include line-engravings, etchings, mezzotints, stipple work, and aquatints. The ink is pressed into the hollows, the paper is first damped, and then passed through the press with the result that the design in ink is transferred from the furrowed plate. Thirdly, must be mentioned Surface Printing, which is neither intaglio nor relief, but consists of obtaining the impressions by contact with the flat stone which has been able to retain the ink : in other words, this is lithography.

Now in regard to colour printing there are two methods, which may be summed up quite briefly as requiring (a) only one plate, (b) several plates, or blocks, or stones. In the former, which is principally confined to intaglio prints, the plate is painted or filled with ink between each printing, the furrows being given the required colour by stumps of rag called " dollies." This manner was to some extent used by seventeenth-century line-engravers, and in a limited degree by mezzotint-engravers. But it was the stipple-engravers who adopted it far more generally. Indeed, it was the introduction of stipple-engraving which caused that conventional and unhappy practice of printing portraits and pretty-pretty drawing-room inanities in brown or brick-red ; and one's memory at once thinks of Angelica Kauffmann (1741—1807).

In the second method, however, the scope is considerably widened to get a more ambitious effect than mere brown or red. It was J. C. Le Blon (1667—1741) who was the first to use in Holland a special process in mezzotint and anticipated the modern three-colour process. He based his scheme on the three cardinal colours red, blue, and yellow, by a combination of which it was possible to get the entire range : that is to say, he obtained his effects by using three separate plates, and by three separate printings he aimed to get on paper an impression that received the whole comprehension of the rainbow's hues. Actually a fourth plate was often required for black or dark greys, and in the late eighteenth century French craftsmen used as many as seven plates, each inked with a different colour. But these were not satisfactory methods, for the greatest nicety was essential in super-imposition if the register was to be obtained with just accuracy. Le Blon was a mezzotinter, yet it cannot be denied that this class of craftsmen refused to allow colour printing to be used for their best plates. The historical fact remains, however, that the printer by covering the plate with various coloured inks was able to produce results not merely from stipple, mezzotint, and line, but from etching, aquatint, wood-engraving and lithography too. Thus an entirely new sphere had been opened which was afterwards to be developed by modern process work.

In due course we shall see in this volume reproductions of colour aquatints, and it is well to realize that such an aquatint rarely received more than two or three colours applied to the plate, but the colouring was largely done afterwards *on the print itself*. For this work young artists (such as Turner), who were in later life to become eminent, were sometimes employed. The method of making a stipple engraving in colour is another matter which will interest us, but we may well appreciate its technique at this stage. Briefly expressed, the incised work on the plate holds the ink, and the non-incised portions print white, the whole essence of stipple-engraving being the presentation of tone by a crowd of dots or flicks. The printer inked the plate with his colour, so that every bit of the furrows in contact with the paper created a corresponding colour effect.

It is true that the eyes of figures and similar important details were afterwards finished on the print by hand, but the emphasis we should keep in mind is that the genuine stipple colour engraving is one that has received its colour from the dabbed plate and not from a hand which afterwards worked on the paper.

For those readers who are sufficiently interested there have been reproduced in a special edition of this volume a series of three prints in colour photogravure, the subjects being respectively: the stipple engraving in colour entitled " The Glorious First of June," by Daniel Orme after Mather Brown; the aquatint in colour of " The Battle off St. Vincent," by and after R. Dodd; and the aquatint in colour of " The Battle of the Nile," also by R. Dodd. Now this modern photogravure process enables such work as stipple and line to be reproduced so accurately that one can hardly distinguish original from copy. The Daniel Orme reproduction is particularly a notable achievement. But the intriguing fact emerges that this twentieth-century photogravure is printed in exactly the same way as the old-fashioned engravings where the colouring was done on the plate. It is an expensive process, for not more than three or four impressions can be done by the printer in a day; but the combination of photography, to obtain on the plate a thin intaglio, together with the individual colouring of the plate, and the printing by handpress, cannot fail to strike us as something unusually attractive. Outside this, however, modern three-colour work is not part of our subject: we are concerned with the ship prints that are old.

It remains to mention a word of warning in connection with pseudo old prints. There are innumerable forgeries and semi-forgeries which have been put on the market in answer to the demand for prints of bygone ships and naval events, and the collector without experience needs to be on his guard. A high-class colour photogravure is in itself a work of art, but pretends to be nothing but the finest reproduction after an original print. The forger of stipple colour-work, on the other hand, colours each impression by hand, thus giving himself away to the collector who has knowledge : for, instead of the non-incised portions of the plate being white (as in the genuine impressions), these have been covered with colour.

Similarly one must beware of coloured mezzotints, for they are in the same category as a worn-out ship whose defects have been disguised with paint. The mezzotint plate may be perfectly genuine, but dating back to the eighteenth century. So many impressions have been made in the meantime that the plate has become worn and capable of printing only weakly. The semi-forger now enters, purchases the plate, prints off the thin impressions, but colours them by hand and offers them to an unsuspecting public. There are several ways for avoiding the danger of being deceived : one is to examine closely beneath the colouring to see the quality of the impression, though in any case, even in the eighteenth century, it was the custom for the worn mezzotint plate to be employed for colour printing. Secondly, as we have seen, a genuine colour print (with the exception of aquatints and a few minute details) is one which has been inked by the printer on the plate and not on the paper. Thirdly, the watermark of the paper can usually date it, though a fake may be printed on genuinely old paper extracted from an antique book. But it is especially by an eye trained through long experience and comparison of prints that any kind of forgery can be detected. This is a matter of time and knowledge, but it is hoped that the following chapters and illustrations of representative examples will suffice to set the amateur on the right lines. Guidance can influence only up to a certain point : from that departure the trained insight and the informed mind must create the essential artistic judgment.

With this introduction we may now proceed to watch the evolution of woodcuts, engravings, etchings, aquatints, mezzo-tints and lithographs in regard to their interpretation of the nautical arts. And by the word "prints" we shall mean the impressions left on paper after having been in contact with the inked surface of the wood, metal or stone.

CHAPTER II

THE FIRST SHIP PRINTS

IT is necessary to begin by transporting ourselves back into the fourteenth century of Central Europe with its guilds of craftsmen ; its castles ; its Gothic churches full of priceless paintings, statuary, and wood carvings ; its monasteries and shrines and pilgrims. First comes the cutter of woodblocks, at the close of that century, who was classed in the guilds with the carpenter, for he is making these types solely for printing patterns on textiles.

Next, with the advent of sufficient paper, we see the woodcut applied for printing pictures of the Passion of our Lord, and of the Saints. These were distributed at various shrines to the pilgrims and were probably the handiwork of monks or conventual sisters. The earliest genuine print is from the wood engraving by Heinecken of St. Christopher, dated 1423, in the Carthusian Convent at Buxheim, but before the use of paper, a very small proportion of early woodcuts had been impressed on vellum. Somewhere before the year 1377 playing cards had been introduced into Germany, though no existing packs of woodcuts can be definitely dated before the middle of the fifteenth century. The earliest date on any print in line-engraving is on one of a series representing the Passion of Christ. This is preserved in Berlin, and is by that anonymous engraver known as " The Master of 1446 " ; yet another craftsman, known as " The Master of the Playing Cards," was working in Upper Germany perhaps ten years before this last-mentioned date.

But it was the invention of printing books that gave the necessary stimulus to engraving. The introduction of movable type occurred just before the middle of the fifteenth century, but the earliest dated documents printed from these types are a couple of " indulgences " (or grants of spiritual privileges in return for alms), which were issued at Mainz in the autumn of 1454. One of these was printed by a goldsmith, and the other by Johann Gutenberg, who had been making experiments with movable type for about the last decade. Then in 1456 came the Gutenberg, or Mazarin, Bible from Mainz, and other fine books followed : but in 1462 occurred the sack of Mainz which for a while caused the dispersion of the printer craftsmen into Cologne, Nuremberg, Ulm and other towns whither the newly-found process was also carried. The result was so immediate that before the century's close there were more than fifty German towns which owned printing presses. Three years after the fall of Mainz two Germans had introduced printing into Italy, so that a hundred and fifty printing firms were at work in Venice alone by the year 1500. Paris received the craft in 1470, the Low Countries by 1473, and three years later William Caxton, who was living as an English Merchant Adventurer in Bruges, learnt to print one or two books in that city. Then, returning to England in 1476, he printed a year later *The Dictes and Sayings of the Philosophers*, which was the first work that ever came from an English press, and was in black letter. As to the " block-books," that is to say those in which both text and illustrations were cut on the wood block, none can be dated before about 1460, but then around this date, or perhaps a couple of years later, arrive the earliest books that contained woodcut illustrations. These were printed by Albrecht Pfister of Bamberg ; but after 1470 woodcut illustrations became common in Germany, and about 1490 common also in Italy. Indeed, until late on into the following century, this method was the most universally employed for reproducing designs, when metal engraving at last superseded it.

But amongst those anonymous fifteenth-century engravers on metal was one who is always known as "The Master W♀," a prolific craftsman who flourished in the Netherlands about the year 1470. He had a wonderful eye for detail, and reproduced a number of engravings showing Gothic architecture. To us he is especially interesting because he left behind an exact print of a ship model. This was a three-masted Flemish carrack, and we thus have one of the most meticulous and accurate sources of information of a contemporary trader such as was wont to sail south to Spain. The print was most likely an exact portrait of some votive offering in a church of Flanders, and quite recently it has again been reconstructed into a model by an English artist who has lent it to the South Kensington Museum. This kind of ship will be referred to again presently.

It was because of the improvement in ship rigs and construction, the extension of trade and travel, the awakening to a desire for geographical knowledge, that there arrived a demand for maps. Now this was not possible to be supplied immediately except by reissue of what was produced over thirteen hundred years previously. In ancient times there had been such cartographers as Posidonius, Hipparchus, Strabo, but the greatest of them all was Claudius Ptolemæus, who made astronomical observations at Alexander in the first half of the second century A.D. His system of geography, containing a description with maps of the known world, actually remained the unquestioned authority down to this fifteenth century. So it was that the earliest maps ever to be printed by the new craft were an edition of Ptolemy's Cosmography in the year 1478. They were issued from the press of Arnold Bukinck at Rome, and were engraved on copper. But the interesting fact emerges that copper engraving for that purpose was not used again until, a hundred years later, we come to Ortelius.

The copper-plate engraver is able to find greater facility for his expression and more definite clearness when reproducing such intricate work as maps : yet, for all that, the wood-cutters competed successfully for this activity, so that in 1482 Leonard Holl at Ulm brought out an edition of the same Cosmography, in which we have the first instance of maps being printed from wood. The cuts were engraved by John Schnitzer, and it requires but little imagination to realize the enormous amount of patient labour in bringing about such an achievement in such material. It is curious that this temporary throw-back should have occurred, but the fact is that the woodcut had already become so firmly established that it was the recognized method. Up till the year 1486, however, all these woodcuts appearing in the printed books consisted of little more than mere outline, the shadows and folds of draperies being indicated by a series of short parallel lines, without the introduction of any lines crossing each other. Thus there was a sense of coldness, a lack of what may be called colour. But with the issue of Breydenbach's *Peregrinationes in Terram Sanctam*, printed in 1486 at Mainz, we have in the frontispiece a woodcut that for the first time employs " cross-hatching," that is to say intersecting parallel lines, for the purpose of adding sunlight and life to the design.

Breydenbach's *Travels*, as an illustrated book, are so remarkable that we may well start with one of its engravings for our detailed study. The first edition was printed in Latin, by or for the artist Erhard Reuwich of Utrecht, and the woodcuts are admitted by the highest critics to be masterpieces of design and execution.

For their fidelity to nature and excellence of finish they are worthy to be compared even with the best examples in their own century, and especially is this in respect of the shipping.

The story is both true and fascinating. Bernhard von Breydenbach was the son of Gerlach von Breydenbach, belonging to an ancient and noble German family. During his youth he lived as recklessly and wildly as many of his age ; but, later, he resolved to make an act of reparation by performing a pilgrimage to the Holy Land, as thousands had done before him with the same object. Bernhard was made a lay Canon of Mainz in 1450, and thirty-three years later he set out on his long travel. Let it be emphasized at once that no one ever undertook such a task lightly or without very careful consideration. It needed not merely money, good health (especially a strong stomach), firm and unflinching determination, but real pluck to sustain the dangers and uncertainties that were awaiting on land as well as sea. A pilgrimage was no pleasant tourist excursion with everything well organized and all obstacles smoothed away beforehand.

It is on record that one Felix Faber went to Eberhard, first Duke of Wurtemberg, as to advice on such a subject, since the Duke had already visited Palestine ; and in answer to Faber's request this is the information that was forthcoming : " There are three things that one cannot advise upon, one way or the other : marriage, war, and the pilgrimage to the Holy Land. They may all begin well and end badly." For, in addition to the weariness of actual journeying, the pilgrims had to suffer extortion at the hands of their transporters and bad food. As we know from other accounts, life on board a pilgrim galley was one long agony of discomfort. Many suffered from sea-sickness, most of them from vermin, all from lack of decent accommodation. There was an utter absence of privacy even for an eminent personage, with neither bench to lie upon nor table from which to eat. The hard deck or your own knees had to suffice for the latter. There were no mattresses, and the passengers lay down to sleep among the blasphemous and abandoned sailors, most of whom were a mixture of the vilest Turks, Albanians, and Macedonians with no hope but death, compelled to serve as galley-slaves as long as life should last.

The skipper of the galley was a martinet over passengers as well as crew, and not above cheating the pilgrims even after having driven a keen bargain. Hard black biscuit full of worms, covered with cobwebs and already gnawed by rats ; hard goat, mutton or beef, rancid lard, and badly cooked, served as food. The drink consisted of filthy water and the kind of wine that was used ashore for dressing salad. In bad weather the passengers were sent below, so as to leave the decks free, and even in fine weather when the wind came ahead and the lateen-yards had to be lowered at each tack and rehoisted. The cries of the sailors on deck and the noise of hurried treads terrified the poor pilgrims below already overcome with nausea. Well earned were the indulgences granted after such trying travels.

Breydenbach's pilgrimage started from the neighbourhood of Mainz on April 25, 1483, accompanied by a hundred and fifty other people, including especially Erhard Reuwich, a painter, who was to make designs of the various places through which they passed. Apart from the fact that he was a really admirable draughtsman we know nothing else either of himself or his work. The expedition, consisting of barons, knights, priests, monastics, scholars, cooks, barbers, stewards, servants, a schoolmaster, and an ex-sailor as language expert, reached Venice in fifteen days and here they met many other pilgrims bound on the same overseas journey. In that Adriatic port, whither came the treasures of the Orient, there was much to hold the attention of Breydenbach and Reuwich whilst they lodged a while in the house of Peter Ugelheymer, a native of Frankfort.

Venice was such a centre of commercial and artistic activity, its citizens were so proud of its achievements, and there was so much sight-seeing to be done by pilgrims who had never previously beheld the sea, or wandered far from the outskirts of Mainz, that the days passed quickly. In the meantime Breydenbach required all his astuteness to bargain with the shipowners, but finally an arrangement was made with Augustino Contarini, who had been skipper of a galley ever since 1471. A contract was now signed by which it was agreed that the galley should arrive at Jaffa within one day of a second vessel, belonging to Peter de Lando, under a penalty of a thousand florins. This condition was to ensure no delay in the passage, since every day afloat meant so much misery to the unfortunate passengers. Inasmuch as Contarini and de Lando were deadly enemies, this competitive clause was all to the good.

It was further agreed that Contarini should provide arms for eighty men since the Mediterranean was the happy cruising area of pirates. Not more than two or three days should be spent at each port unless departure was delayed by weather. The pilgrims were to be given two meals a day, consisting of good bread, good wine, fresh meat, and eggs ; but, also, some more bread and wine as a refection and collation in the morning and evening. If any of the pilgrims died before reaching the Holy Land, then half of the deceased's passage money was to be refunded. The skipper was to provide an interpreter at his own expense as far as Jaffa and back, but it was also stipulated that only one half of the fares should be paid at Venice, the remainder being settled when Jaffa was actually reached. The cost of transporting a passenger varied from 20 ducats in 1470 to 55 ducats in 1480.

Thus after twenty-two days had been spent wandering through

Venice visiting the churches and sacred relics, whilst Reuwich drew his sketches of the architecture and shipping, and the pilgrims had been impressed by the information that was freely given by the Venetians concerning the latter's readiness for war, the party went aboard Contarini's and de Lando's craft. Well might the Mainz travellers marvel that 600 war galleys could be made ready for the Adriatic within a few days, and that within only a few hours 200,000 men could be summoned for defence of the Republic; that at least 1,000 men were always employed at the arsenal making artillery, and fifty women busy making sails. But apart from all this military activity these voyagers from Central Europe were able to see how brisk the port was with merchant ships arrived from such distant parts as Alexandria, Damascus, Barbary, Constantinople, Jaffa, Flanders, and England. Just, however, as everything was ready for the pilgrims' departure there was a sudden set-back. Contarini was arrested for debt and it seemed as if, after every contingency had been provided against, the expedition would get no further.

But matters were eventually adjusted, the two pilgrim galleys got under way on June 1, went across to the east side of the Adriatic and reached the old Roman harbour of Parenzo. Here they stayed till June 3 and got to Corfu on the 12th. After three days they were off again, called at Modon on the south-west coast of Greece, and by the 18th of the month they were at Rhodes. From very early times this had been a place of commercial prosperity, it had passed through so many vicissitudes, was now the headquarters of the Knights Hospitallers, and only three years previous to Breydenbach's visit the Turks had besieged and damaged it. The pilgrims found opportunity to visit the church and relics, but Contarini saw that the voyage was resumed on the 22nd. Cyprus was made in four days, and here they remained less than twenty-four hours. Another three days at sea passed and then the Palestine coast was sighted. Thus Contarini was able to bring them safely into Jaffa, and de Lando's galley soon followed.

The rest of the journey need not detain us long. All the pilgrims got to Jerusalem, whence some of them proceeded to Mount Sinai and returned home *via* Alexandria. Breydenbach, who was the originator and moving spirit of the whole pilgrimage, arrived back at the end of January 1484. In that same year he was made Dean of Mainz Cathedral, and lived till 1497, when he was buried in this very church, his body being embalmed with spices that he had brought from the East.

Now, fortunately for our interest and pleasure, Breydenbach on getting back from his pilgrimage took steps to have this account printed in Mainz, which had been the birthplace of Gutenberg. The text was written in Latin, not by Breydenbach himself but by a Dominican named Martin Roth, a distinguished doctor of divinity, who had not accompanied the expedition. This publication was in effect a tourist guide likely to assist any others who might think of making the pilgrimage to the East. It was indeed destined to become so popular that it was translated into German, Flemish, and French, and between 1486 and 1522 no fewer than a dozen editions appeared. Containing such data as the distances from Venice to the various places *en route* to Jaffa ; much information concerning the Holy Land, the manners, rites, and errors of those in whose possession it happened still to be held ; with such miscellaneous matter as Mohammedan laws, remedies for sea-sickness (handed down from two Arabian physicians who flourished in the tenth and twelfth centuries respectively), and remedies against vermin, it was the very book that was required.

Roth's text matches the woodcuts, all of which were drawn by Reuwich, though we cannot say who was the actual engraver. They consist of panoramic views of the places visited, figures of strange animals, and various Oriental alphabets. Not merely were these panoramic views the first ever made on such a large size, but never previously had one single painter been known to undertake the illustration of a printed book. They are of the greatest importance because they were actually sketched on the spot, authentic, artistic. Many of the other woodcut views belonging to the fifteenth century are not authentic, as we shall presently find; whereas Reuwich has left for all time an exact picture of famous places as seen in 1483, and the earliest printed representations known of Venice, Parenzo, Modon, Corfu, and Rhodes.

Reproduced as Plate 2 in this book is Reuwich's lively illustration of Rhodes. In the middle distance we can see the chain boom to defend the harbour and its shipping from any sudden arrival of the enemy, and the artist has shown the unrepaired heavy damage which the Turks had wrought on this stronghold three years previously. In the foreground is the two-masted galley in which Breydenbach and his fellow-pilgrims were transported by Contarini from Venice to Jaffa. This galley is, of course, lateen-rigged, the mainsail being far the bigger, and the woodcut clearly shows a couple of hands at the peak end of the yard engaged in stowing the sail under the supervision of an officer who stands half-way down the yard. This spar is correctly shown to consist of two pieces lashed together in accordance with historic custom obtaining in the Mediterranean. At the masthead is clearly shown the top from which darts and other missiles could be hurled against any ship that dared to attack.

Coming down on deck and looking from forward to aft we note the banner which flies at the bows. This bears the device of the Jerusalem cross of the pilgrims. At the stern are two more flags, which have been thought to represent Burgundy and Flanders, whilst on the awning is the Lion of St. Mark which Contarini would naturally be proud to display. There are many interesting points in this galley worthy of attention ; such for instance as the survival of the ram, the hawse pipes and stowage of the anchors, the pens just forward of the mizzen mast for carrying the pilgrims' horses. Then, again, Reuwich has shown such details as the single-fluked grappling anchor to be used in tackling and boarding an enemy, the canvas screens for keeping out the seas from the oarsmen, whilst there are such items of gear indicated as the block and vangs of the mizzen, the top cranes with their crane-lines for hoisting up further supplies of darts or stones to be hurled from the maintop.

Inside the chain-protected harbour the artist has tried to give the reader an idea of the three-masted ship lying under protection of the walls ; but, inasmuch as the latter interfere with the rigging, he has shown us in the open sea a three-master at anchor, running before the wind, and on a wind across the horizon. This ship is the conventional carrack of the time, and Reuwich has given a more impressionistic idea of that class whose model was reproduced by " The Master W✠." There can be no doubt but that both artists were contemplating the same type of vessel which was well known as a trader from the Levant to the North Sea. She is the typical fifteenth-century big-bellied round ship, with rounded forefoot and full round stern. The fore and after " castles " are seen as the usual fighting platforms, super-imposed on the ship's hull, but soon to be embodied in the actual design.

As to the rig, we are able to witness the transition stage from the single-sail type handed down from Viking times ; for, if this fifteenth-century vessel carries three sails, it is really the large main-sail that matters, the foresail and mizzen being used on a wind, as shown, but rather as auxiliaries. Presently the latter were to become of increased importance. The bowsprit, correctly shown as well-steeved, was as yet primarily for the purpose of supporting the stays and bowlines, in addition to suspending the grapnel, which could thus be dropped from a height on to the enemy's decks when boarding tactics should begin. Reuwich has carefully indicated the powerful rigging for the mainmast and the important round-top with its supply of darts kept in readiness. Thus, in short, by representing in one picture both a carrack and a galley he has given us the two opposite types along which naval architecture developed : the long, quick-manœuvring, shallow craft, and the short, round, more seaworthy, deeper draught vessel able to carry the maximum amount of cargo.

I have stressed these Reuwich-Breydenbach prints because it is difficult to exaggerate their importance to the collector of nautical material. So much was the artist a pioneer that others did not fail to borrow his first-hand designs unblushingly. It will suffice to give three instances. The great Venetian painter Carpaccio, who displayed in his works such minute knowledge of Oriental costumes and figures that it has been assumed he visited the East, used three of Reuwich's figures of Saracens and Abyssinians in painting the Triumph of St. George in the chapel of San Giorgio degli Schiavoni, Venice. Secondly, Reuwich's work becomes associated with Christopher Columbus in a strange manner. The latter set out for his memorable first voyage across the western ocean in 1492, and after discovering the Bahamas, Cuba and Hispaniola, got back to Europe in the following year. In 1493 was translated his famous *Epistola de insulis nuper repertis*, giving an account of his initial voyage. This is a very rare book nowadays, and in 1494 there was an edition issued at Basle containing four woodcuts, of which the first and the last are absolute " cribs," having nothing whatsoever to do with Columbus's *Santa Maria* or his other two ships,

Pinta and *Nina.* For the first of the four cuts is a galley! Quite
apart from her unsuitability for crossing the Atlantic, this illustration has been copied from Reuwich's pilgrim galley seen in our
reproduction. The only alteration which the Basle engraver made
was to reverse it, remove the obvious Jerusalem flag at the bows,
and then let the cut go at that. The horses in the pens, and everything else aboard, are presented just as observed off Rhodes.
Similarly the last of the Basle quartette shows an excellent stern
view of such a fifteenth-century carrack as we discussed just now.
It is true that the Basle printer has this design reversed also, but
in all other respects it is exactly as appeared in Reuwich's design
showing the port and shipping of Modon. The third instance of
plagiarism will be noted in the following chapter.

The various editions of Breydenbach are eagerly sought, and the
accompanying print has been taken from that of 1502 printed by
Drach at Speier. This Gothic-lettered book was the third Latin
edition. The French translation of Breydenbach by N. Huen,
folio, printed at Lyons in 1488, beginning, " A tres haulte tres
cretienne et tres redoubtee princesse," was the first French book
to appear with copper plates, and during the first half of the nineteenth century fetched £84. Obviously it is worth considerably
more nowadays. But we pass on to examine a coloured woodcut.

CHAPTER III

SHIPPING AND ENGRAVING

OF all the old romantic towns in Europe few appeal to us with such fascination as the walled and moated Nuremberg, which still remains in respect of its mediæval buildings and its art treasures one of the richest in the world. From its position on the route between the Netherlands and Venice it necessarily became an important centre of activity and thought. The industry of its inhabitants was proverbial, and as the place became a free township in the thirteenth century there was every encouragement for the work of hand and brain in a brotherhood of peace and an atmosphere of contentment.

Under such happy conditions the arts and crafts prospered amazingly. Painting and sculpture, wood-carving and music, engraving and printing were fostered by their guilds, and one inevitably thinks of Wagner's Mastersingers, of Hans Sachs, Beckmesser, Walther von Stolzing and the rest. For it was at the close of the fifteenth and the beginning of the next century that the guilds had reached their climax, and under the prudent discipline of the older men there grew up such painters and engravers as Dürer, the greatest of all designers in woodcuts, Hans Sebald Beham, George Pencz, and other masters, who were in turn to hand on the tradition to their successors; as Peter Visscher, the Nuremberg sculptor, did to his five eminent sons, all of whom became skilled with their chisels.

Thus, confining ourselves immediately to book production, we can hardly be surprised at the ambitious work which Nuremberg issued in 1493 under the title *Registrum hujus operis libri cronicarum*. This " Chronicon Norimbergense " was originally issued in two editions, the first in Latin and the second in German a few months later. The latter is even more scarce than the other, and even fifty years ago fetched from £15 to £30. The perfect collection of prints can never be complete without at least one of the woodcuts which the *Nuremberg Chronicle* contains. This great folio was compiled by its contemporary Hartmann Schedel, a Nuremberg physician ; its illustrations of cities and figures of people were executed under the superintendence of Michael Wohlgemuth and of William Pleydenwurff, who were reputed as mathematicians as well as painters—" adhibitis tamen viris mathematicis pingendique arte peritissimis " is the description applied to these art-editors, as we may regard them. Now Wohlgemuth was that master to whom Dürer in his early career was apprenticed, and the book was issued by Anthony Koburger, the famous printer, who was Dürer's godfather. Thus we have the closest connection between the ablest artists and the most skilled reproducers of that day.

Certainly the *Nuremberg Chronicle* is a curious collection both as to letterpress and woodcuts. There is an excellent copy of the Latin edition in the British Museum, and as we turn over its leaves we may feel inclined to smile at the ponderous German mentality. But here are distinguished literary and artistic men of the fifteenth century trying to quicken the minds of their fellow-townsmen towards the big fundamentals of life. In a sense it is a kind of picture-book, for there are about two thousand woodcuts, most of them being half-page ; but it is less an encyclopædia than a guide to knowledge. The book opens with the creation of the world, and there is an arresting cut showing Noah's ark in course of construction. Inasmuch as these inland dwellers had knowledge only of the conventional fifteenth-century carrack type, the ark is drawn as just such a vessel, with fighting forecastle and sterncastle of the type already seen in Reuwich's Rhodes design. Those Nurembergers with their lack of information, which can come only from original research, could not possibly know what even an Egyptian ship of the Dynastic period resembled ; and though to-day no artist could reconstruct Noah's craft, yet the last thing he would do would be to depict a three-masted sailing ship of his own period.

But we must not be too critical, for the compilers were doing their best. If to-day an instructor going into the heart of Wiltshire, or the Middle West of America, tried to show landsmen, who had never left their farms, what Noah's ship actually resembled in appearance, he would have no easier task than Wohlgemuth and Pleydenwurff faced. The Chronicle has less regard for originality of conception than for an employment of the limited material at its disposal, so that the results are often amusing. Some of the designs were unmistakably adapted from the Reuwich-Breydenbach publication, and there is a strange disregard for historical accuracy. Thus you will find large woodcuts intended to indicate Jerusalem and Damascus, yet with the Mediæval Gothic churches and steeples of Germany. Similarly, when the art-editors ran short of blocks for one town, they used again the same which had done duty for another. In this way the wood-cut of Damascus serves on other pages for such different localities as Neapolis and Perugia.

The large double-page illustration of Venice is " lifted " from Breydenbach, and further on at the back of folio LI comes the illustration reproduced here as a colour frontispiece. This purports to be the ancient city of Tarvisium, more familiar to us under the name of Treviso, which lies eighteen miles north of Venice.

It is true that Treviso already possessed its fifteenth-century cathedral and the Gothic church of Santa Maddalena, but there was no reason (so far as the editors were concerned) why this design should not be given whatever geographical title was most convenient. That which chiefly entertains us, however, is the three-masted carrack which is shown outside the city's walls. This has been copied from Reuwich's carrack in the Rhodes woodcut, but it has been reversed. Three sailors on the mainyard and one other below it on deck have been added for the Nuremberg block, but otherwise the two ships are practically the same down to the very angles at which the yards have been lowered and crossed.

Throughout the Chronicle there are other woodcuts which also reveal the round-bellied ships with military maintop. There are seamen going about their duties, there are harbour-quays and so on, all of these details contributing to our nautical knowledge of that century. It is, none the less, something of a shock to find before the end of the book that a cut which pretends to represent Magdeburg is in fact identically that which has also served for Treviso. The book contains a large double-page print of Nuremberg, which is perhaps the finest thing of the whole series ; for there was no necessity here to plagiarize. But the towers, the spires, and embattlements of the engravers' own beloved city are shown with an enthusiastic fidelity and truthfulness.

The introduction of cross-hatching gave to these woodcuts a warmth and tone which make them of greater attractiveness, yet they are lacking in spirit and feeling when compared with much of the other fifteenth-century engraving. The *Nuremberg Chronicle* artists have sought to obtain their effects by strongly marked shadows cut in stout contiguous lines. Many of these cuts, however, show that the editors were anxious to give their uncritical public rather a large quantity of entertaining illustrations than a few selected impressions of the highest excellence. As one critic of the nineteenth century reminds us, these are to be appreciated not for their art but their imagery. And at a time when Europe was beginning to wake up from its long Mediæval slumber and inquire concerning the world about it, the *Nuremberg Chronicle* and later volumes supplied part of the same pleasure which in our own time is obtained from the illustrated newspapers. The map which the compilers included in this volume is of further interest as showing how limited was fifteenth-century geographical knowledge. Anglia is indicated with London (Lvndea) marked, as also shown are Ireland (Ibernia), Scotland (Scocia), Iceland (Vslant) ; but the full burst of enlightenment had yet to come.

A further confirmation of what we can now readily accept from " The Master W♣," from Reuwich, and the *Nuremberg Chronicle* as the standardized type of ocean-going merchantship will be found in the next print. Here we have a couple of such vessels in an engagement off the coast of Iceland. This is taken from a book written by Olaus Magnus (1496–1558), Archbishop of Upsala, concerning the North European peoples. Like many other books of the time it was printed in Latin, the title being *Historia de Gentibus Septentrionalibus*, the incident shown bearing the explanation, " De mutua strage mercatorum pro portubus Islandiae." This volume, which is full of many quaint chapters on wars, winds, whales and much else, appeared at Rome in 1555, but another edition was printed, also in Latin, at Antwerp three years later. In 1658 there was printed at London, in English, a version entitled, " *A Compendious History of the Goths, Swedes and Vandals and Other Northern Nations*, written by Olaus Magnus, Arch-Bishop of Upsall and Metropolitan of Sweden."

It is by piecing together data such as are gathered by these early publications that we can fill in the gaps and get a fairly full picture of past seafaring. From the Archbishop's account we have positive information of the jealousies and fights which went on between the merchant ships of Bremen, Lubeck, Scotland and England for the primacy of the sea and the privilege of riding at anchor in Icelandish harbours. The book tells us of " the leather ships made of hides used by the Pyrats of Greenland " ; " of the manner of fishing for whales " ; and we get an insight as to the early sixteenth-century

ENGAGEMENT BETWEEN TWO MERCHANT SHIPS OFF THE COAST OF ICELAND.
From an engraving of 1555.

mariner by the regulation which insisted that any who " shall perniciously falsify the marriner's compass, especialy the needle " was to lose one of his hands. Having regard to the enormity of such an offence against the safety of ship and crew, the penalty was obviously well deserved.

In this print of the merchantmen bombarding each other it will be noticed that as they are running before the wind neither foresail nor mizzen is set. The ship to starboard has two guns mounted aft, and is able to deliver a broadside of eight. The use of artillery in Northern European ships had already during the first half of the sixteenth century made considerable progress. Portholes had been introduced into the English ships during the reign of Henry VII, and although shot of iron, lead and stone were the ammunition, yet there was still great reliance on boarding tactics and therefore on bows, arrows, spears, pikes, halberds and bills. Indeed, as William Bourne wrote in the year immediately preceding the Armada operations, "We English men have not beene counted but of last daies to become good Gunners"; for the art of using naval guns which would fire a 30-lb. ball had been regarded by our forefathers as a " barbarous and rude thing." The extreme range of such a ball was less than 2,800 yards fired by a demi-cannon; but supposing these Icelandish merchants carried only " periers " they could fire a 24-lb. ball about a hundred yards less. We must not expect too much detailed accuracy from the draughtsman : for instance he has omitted in both ships to show the bowsprit. But as illustrating northern cargo vessels of a date immediately preceding the Elizabethan period these prints are helpful and we are glad to have our slender resources strengthened.

Perhaps the most modern item in the book is the line engraving, also here reproduced, showing a contemporary lifebelt which is discussed in a chapter, "De natatione armati militis." Sixteenth-century books dealing with bright ideas, and what the seaman of to-day terms " gadgets," were not unknown. The same William Bourne, for instance, in 1578 published a little volume entitled *Inventions or Devises Very necessary for all Generalles and Captaines, or Leaders of men, as well by Sea as by Land*, which contained useful tips for preventing an enemy boarding, how to sink him when he was in superior strength, and so on. Bourne even suggested a method how " you may make a Boate to goe without oares or Sayle, by the placing of certaine wheels on the outside

of the Boate, in that sort, that the armes of the wheeles may goe into the water, and so turning the wheeles by some provision, and so the wheeles shall make the Boate to goe." In other words, here was an Elizabethan already thinking ahead towards the solution which was found in the nineteenth-century steamship.

But the Swedish Archbishop's " gadget " was a method of enabling even a soldier in armour to keep afloat by means of a leather bag filled with air (" saccus coriarius insuflatus ") by means of a pipe (" fistula "). The design here shows the bag or belt below the soldier's arms and supported by straps across the shoulders, whilst he is in the act of

SIXTEENTH-CENTURY LIFEBELT.
From an engraving of 1555.

inflating it. To many who served afloat in the British Navy during the recent Great War this print will be reminiscent of almost identically the same article which was in use at the Dardanelles and elsewhere. The book, altogether, is so replete with maritime incidents and illustrations—not excluding the sea-serpent—that the collector will find it a great joy.

Israhel van Mechenem of Bocholt, who died in 1503, whose father has been identified with *The Master of the Berlin Passion*, was another early line engraver by whose work we get yet further illuminative details of the late fifteenth-century ships. Frans Huys, who made engravings of the younger Pieter Breughel's

(Page 23)

BREYDENBACH'S PILGRIM GALLEY AT RHODES,
1483. *Woodcut after the design by* ERHARD REUWICH.

PLATE 2

(Page 36)

PORT OF GENOA. *From a contemporary Italian line engraving.* **1573.**

PLATE 3

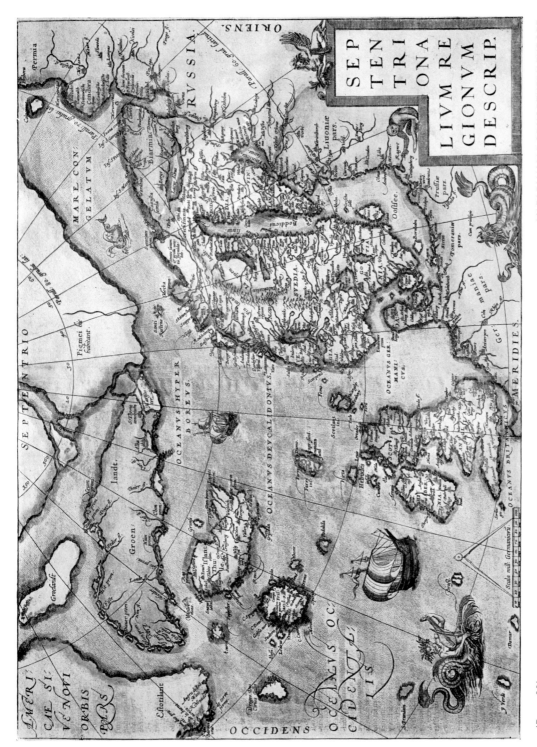

(Page 39)

AN EARLY MAP OF NORTHERN EUROPE.
From Ortelius' Atlas of 1570.

PLATE 4

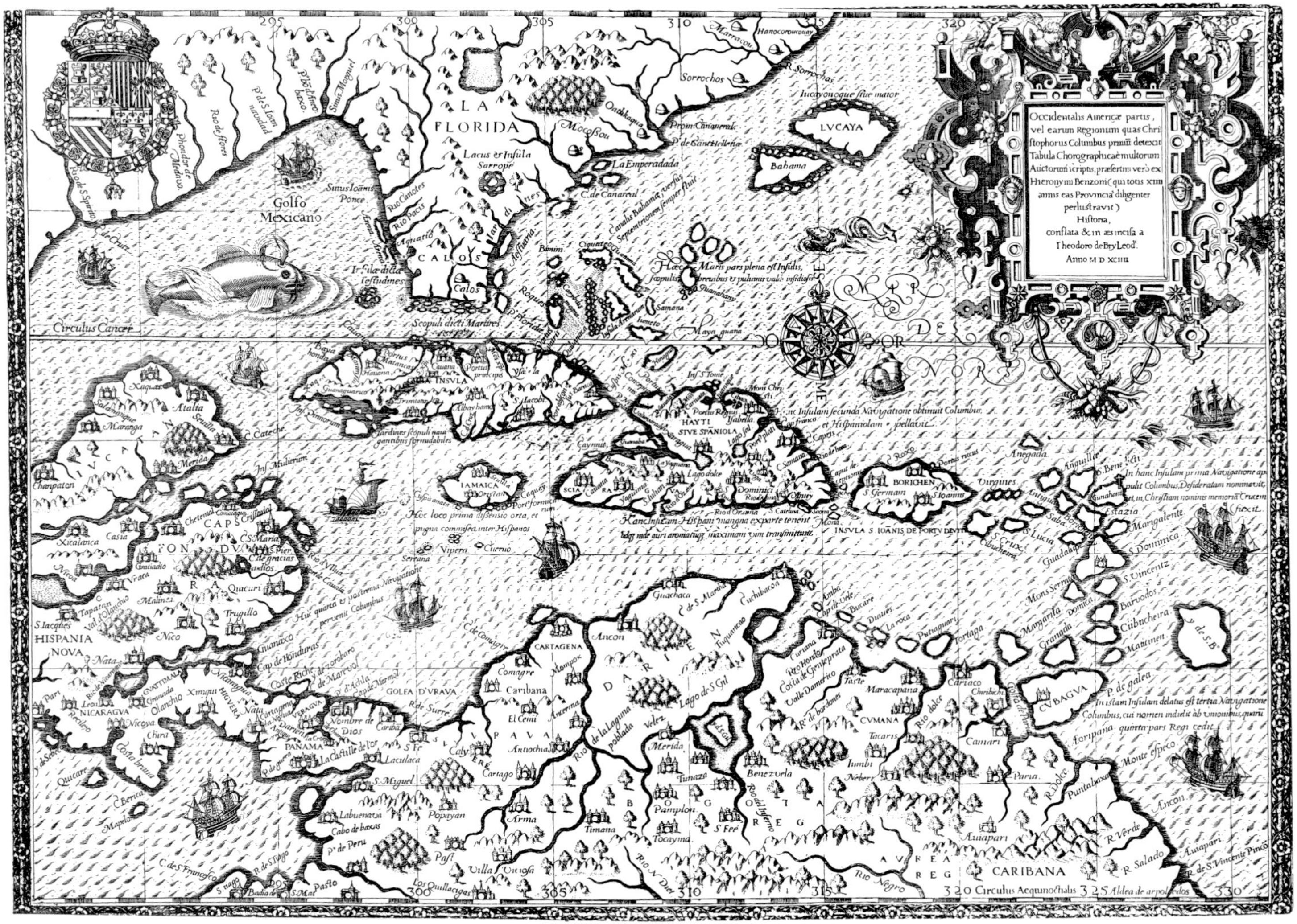

(Page 47)

AN EARLY MAP OF THE WEST INDIES AND CARIBBEAN.
Engraved by THEODORE DE BRY, and printed in 1594

PLATE 5

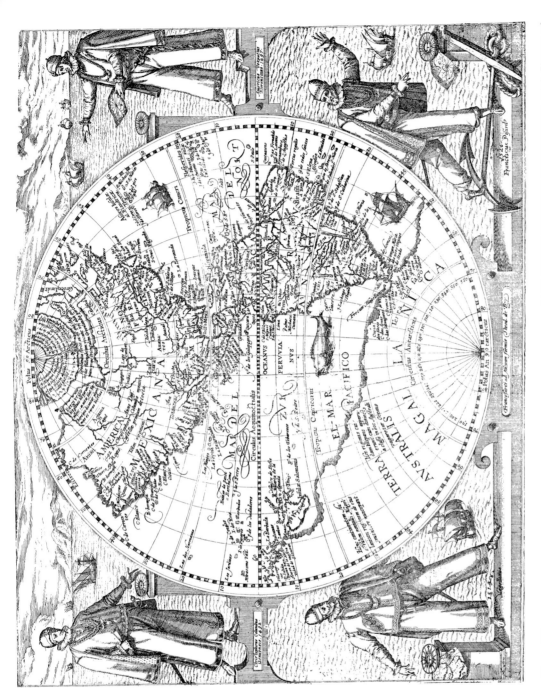

(Page 48)

MAP OF THE WESTERN HEMISPHERE. *With Figures of*
COLUMBUS, VESPUCIUS, MAGELLAN *and* DRAKE.
Engraved by THEODORE DE BRY *in* 1596.

PLATE 6

(Page 48)   STADE AT CAPE DE GEL. *Engraved by* THEODORE DE BRY, 1592.

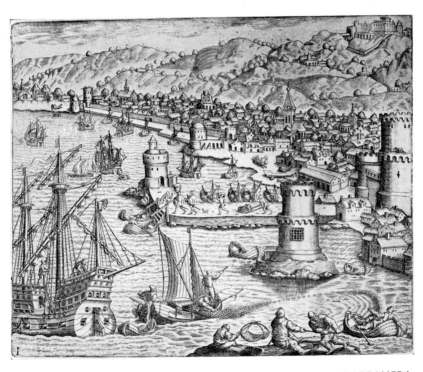

(Page 49)   BENZON REACHES SAN LUCAR DE BARRAMEDA. *Engraved by* THEODORE DE BRY, 1594.

PLATE 7

(Page 50)   BENZON'S SHIP AMONG THE FLYING FISH.
                          Engraved by THEODORE DE BRY, 1594.

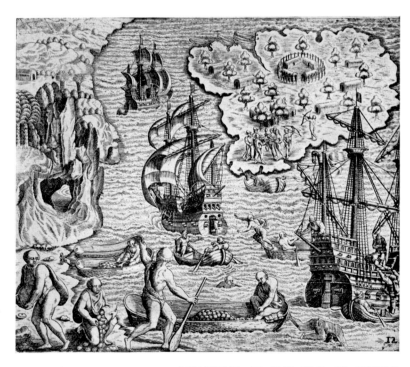

(Page 51)   COLUMBUS AT THE ISLE OF PEARLS.
                          Engraved by THEODORE DE BRY, 1594.

                                                         PLATE 8

(Page 51)
THE SPANIARDS AT MARGARITA ISLAND.
Engraved by THEODORE DE BRY, 1594.

CHRISTOPHORVS COLVMBVS LIGVR. *terroribus Oceani superatis alterius pene Orbis regiones à se inventas Hispaniæ regibus addixit. An. salutis* ᴐᴐ.VIIII.

(Page 52)
THE DREAM OF COLUMBUS. *Engraved by*
THEODORE DE BRY, 1594.

PLATE 9

sixteenth-century Dutch warships, rigged with three and even four masts, has left for our study just those historical characteristics and particulars which the ship-lover longs to find. There are the lofty castles forward and aft, the bonnets to the courses, the protective shields, the netting at the waist to prevent boarding ; the guns of heavy, medium and small sizes ; the lateen sail on the mizzen mast, and much else to be examined with care. The amateur will find occasionally a contemporary ship used as an embellishment on the title-page of a late sixteenth-century book, and there are much more finished shipping prints by the Dutch engraver Cornelius Danckerts, who was born in 1561. It is true that the latter part of the sixteenth and the early years of the seventeenth centuries were not a distinguished period of engravers, yet these practitioners attained a great technical standard and a considerable output, owing to the demand for adorning the increasing number of books which were now being printed. Antwerp was especially a busy centre, and there was a great demand also for portraits. In England the earliest dated copper-plate engravings begin from 1540, when there was issued from the press of the printer-physician, Thomas Raynald, *The Byrth of Mankynde* ; for most of the first English copper-plate craftsmen were illustrators employed for the booksellers. They had settled in London from the Netherlands and taught our ancestors that which had so long been prospering abroad.

The earliest known example of these settlers was Thomas Geminus, a Flemish surgeon at the court of Henry VIII, and he was working about the period 1553 in Blackfriars, as a printer. It was, however, that marvellous sea-fever, that later sixteenth-century zest for ocean travel and discovery, which gave the greatest possible demand for books of illustrated voyages, and for maps showing the explored territories. Hence such engravers as the van de Passe family of Utrecht, six in number, either lived in England for quite considerable periods or engraved large numbers of English subjects. Simon and Willem van de Passe, sons of Crispin van de Passe, both were employed over here during the reign of James I. Simon, who did portraits of Edward VI, Henry Prince of Wales, Sir Walter Raleigh, Captain John Smith, and maps, lived in England for ten years from 1616, finally dying at Copenhagen. Unquestionably this family exercised great influence on engraving in England, but there was now to grow up an English school which was to do much in spreading the enthusiasm for maritime activity, for overseas adventure ; for trade with India, and colonization across the Atlantic in the West Indies, as well as Virginia and New England. Thus, the relationship between English engraving and English shipping was from the first most intimate. In Italy woodcuts had come into use at a date later than their introduction into Germany, and practically little is known of such southern craftsmen till after the fifteenth century, though Venice knew such artists as Jacopo de' Barbari and Niccolo Boldrini in the period between about 1450 and 1566. When we come to working on metal we find also that whereas line-engraving was being practised in Germany before 1446 there is reason to suppose it was adopted by Italy rather after than before this date. The greatest, and certainly one of the earliest, Italian line-engravers was the famous painter Andrea Mantegna (1431— 1506). Jacopo de' Barbari, just mentioned, worked also on metal, and there was Marcantonio Raimondi (c. 1480—1530), who is worthy to be mentioned in the same class as Dürer ; but during the sixteenth century there were in Mantua, Parma, Rome, and Venice miscellaneous other Italian line-engravers.

Of this work an instance is afforded by the preceding Plate 2 of Genoa, which was printed at Rome in 1573. Well might the engraver inscribe on the plate " nobilissima citta," since Genoa already had done great things for the promotion of seafaring and raised up a mighty race of sailors. Not the least of her sons was Christopher Columbus himself ; but even during the twelfth century she had become a powerful maritime state. Able to take part in the Crusades, establishing settlements in the Levant, defeating her great rival Pisa but crippled by her other rival Venice, she none the less went on to make Genoese merchants rich because of the great galleys and tall ships which used this port. Hence, during the sixteenth century, her citizens were able to rear such handsome and palatial buildings and churches.

These the engraver has indicated with topographical care, and the design is characteristic of the next hundred years : the aim being to provide an illustrative survey which combined the advantages of a map and a picture. Thus the breakwaters with the recognized anchorage, the piers and prominent landmarks, would easily be identified and the mariner would have no anxiety in piloting his vessel. A compass card has been engraved, and there are careful embellishments of the two contemporary types of ship, viz. the Mediterranean galley with its lateen sail and oars, and the three-masted big-bodied carrack, square-rigged with topsails. Such a craft as the latter was especially the merchants' friend since several hundred tons of commerce could be carried between Northern Europe and the Eastern Mediterranean. It is, however, interesting to note that this conscientious artist has not omitted even those sprit-rigged little open boats which, through the influence chiefly of the Netherlands, were to develop the fore-and-aft rig illustrated in a subsequent chapter.

Thus, with Germany, the Netherlands, and Italy now at work on metal plates, the New Learning was able to hand on for posterity those great maritime traditions which had been so long in building up, and were to be reinterpreted by successive generations in more perfect ships.

CHAPTER IV

ART AND ADVENTURE

The marvellous explosion of pent-up sea energy in the six-teenth century was the result of the pressure which had been going on during those years which coincide with the early efforts of the engravers.

When in the year 1415 Prince Henry the Navigator retired from the world to found his nautical university at Sagres, he was in fact laying down the basis of knowledge on which, presently, practical seamen were to carry out their adventures. For forty-five years this pioneer in theory was educating and inspiring mariners with the grand aim of finding for Portugal a sea route to the rich East Indies. But from this new-born zeal there developed in the mind of Christopher Columbus even as early as 1474 the notion that the way might be found, not by going east about, but west across the Atlantic. Every one knows that at last he set out in August 1492, that he discovered the Bahamas, Cuba, Haiti which he named Hispaniola, and was back in Europe by the following spring. It was this sudden revealing of the New World to Mediæval Europe, steeped as the latter still was in unprogressive parochialism, that gave the first shock which incited the stay-at-homes to consider the sea.

Then, after Vasco da Gama by the eastern route had attained the Indies in 1498, there sailed Ferdinand Magellan, the Portuguese, westward over the Atlantic swell to Brazil, discovering the straits that now bear his name ; and breaking into the seclusion of the Pacific, he sped on till he had proved, before the first quarter of the sixteenth century had passed, that the world could be circumnavigated. In these two startling and tremendous achievements, intensified by the second and third voyages of Columbus, and subsequently by Drake's round-the-globe voyage of 1577—1580, there was all the requisite surprise to make Europe gasp, to send inquiring minds towards a study of geography and a desire for maps. In the meantime the Spanish colonization of Haiti, the voyages of Hawkins and Drake into the forbidden Caribbean ; the great poverty in England and need for overseas expansion ; the influence of that lecturer and compiler Richard Hakluyt (1552–1616) with his belief in the value of naval history as a means of encouraging others to go forth and venture ; were all still further emphasizing the need to know more of those lands which were reached by ships and the sea. It was thus that cartographers were called on to produce maps, and the engravers were called in to reproduce them.

Already we have seen, as far back as 1478, a demand for Ptolemy's very stale and extremely inadequate *Cosmography* to be reissued drawn on copper plates. Then came that phase of wood-cutting until in 1570 Abraham Ortelius, the great geographer and mathematician of Antwerp, published his important atlas, entitled *Theatrum Orbis Terrarum*, five years before he was to be appointed geographer to Philip II of Spain, whose Armada at a later date was to invade English waters. Under Ortelius' superintendence this collection of maps—the first really great and comprehensive book on modern geography—was engraved not in wood but in copper ; and so great was their excellence when compared with existing maps in wood, that within a few years the entire activity of cartographical reproduction became the work of copper-engravers exclusively.

I have here included from Ortelius' atlas his map of Northern

Europe, which is more than instructive as showing the state of
geographical knowledge thirty years before the end of the century.
This, like nearly all the maps in the atlas, was engraved by
Franz Hogenberg, who lived some time in Mechlin and Cologne.
The disproportions and inaccuracies of the cartographer will be
immediately visible : even the Shetlands and the Faroes are shown
on too great a scale. Concerning the waters north of Iceland's
latitude information had been obtained partly from the whalers ;
but the whole area westward of Anglia and Hibernia was necessarily based on the slenderest details available from unscientific
navigators equipped with totally inadequate instruments. It is,
however, very helpful when we read of the early sixteenth-century
voyages to have in mind such maps as this ; and our admiration for
the venturesome faith of those who sailed through dark nights and
boisterous days over uncharted seas increases magnificently.

The collector will find it possible to pick up both Ortelius' atlas
itself and odd maps from this series. They are not without their
decorative attraction in colour, and in any case well worth careful
consideration. Franz Hogenburg's life is covered by the period
1558—1590, or nearly the whole of Elizabeth's reign. But it was
Gerard Mercator who did so much towards the practical perfection
of maps for the use of seafarers. Ortelius (or Ortell) was born in
1527 and died in 1598. Mercator (whose real name was Kremer)
lived from 1512 to 1592. A Fleming who first saw light in Rupel-
monde, Mercator was appointed cosmographer or map-maker to
the Duke of Cleves in 1552, his chief work being his great atlas
begun in 1585, though it was not till four years after his death that
his engravings appeared in collected form. His " Mappemonde,"
containing a method of projecting a sphere on a plane, had been
issued to the world in 1569. It is by this invention, according to
which marine charts are still drawn, that his fame will always live.

Jodocus Hondius was another of those Flemish engravers who did excellent service in graving maps on copper. He was not born till 1563, and his son Hendrick carried on his work after him. There were, too, Wagenaer's plans of Dutch harbours and the Narrow Seas which were so valuable to the mariner that an English version had soon to be issued. Lucus Wagenaer had published his atlas at Leyden in 1585, and herein was set forth graphically that accumulation of knowledge respecting the soundings and sandbanks which had been obtained by expert pilots as they sailed out of Dutch harbours, up the Thames estuary and elsewhere.

It has ever been the genius of the English nation not so much to invent as to improve rapidly on the inventions of others. The nineteenth and twentieth centuries are as full of general instances, as the previous generations were of special exemplifications, in regard to better shipbuilding methods learned from the Dutch and the French. But in the realm of engraving the seventeenth century was characterized by the manner in which the English first sent to the Continent for the best craftsmen ; then by the way in which the skill was learned and developed, until there became a real English school.

Both Remigius and Franz Hogenberg crossed the North Sea to London after 1570, Jodocus Hondius arrived in 1583, and they were all kept busy engraving maps as well as portraits and topographical views in response to the new learning and the renaissance of geographical study. After his sojourn here Hondius went back to Amsterdam, where he died in 1612. The nature of his work is readily understood when one remembers that it included four maps for illustrating Sir Francis Drake's West Indian voyage, published at Leyden in 1588 ; the well-known portrait of Drake entitled " Franciscvs Draeck Nobilissimvs Eqves Angliæ " ; some plates for *The Mariner's Mirror* (the English version of Wagenaer's atlas), as well as for John Speed's important English atlas, *Theatre of the Empire of Great Britain*. Hondius in signing his plates sometimes added a barking hound, in punning reference to his own name, with the motto " sub cane vigilante."

But the earliest use by foreign craftsmen working in England, of line-engraving for geographical illustration is found in a double-page map of the Holy Land in the second folio edition of the Bishops' Bible, printed in 1572, which contains also the embellishment of ships and a whale. The map was engraved by Humphrey Cole, though the frontispiece was done probably by Franz Hogenberg. The first traceable name in a native English school was that of Augustine Ryther. He was born at Leeds, but exactly when it is impossible to state. Certainly he was flourishing between 1575 and 1592, and it is further believed that he died soon after that last-mentioned date. Ryther kept a print-seller's shop near Leadenhall, where he was associated with Christopher Saxton in the engraving and publishing of county maps. We are especially interested in Ryther for having engraved a set of double-folio plates under the title, " Expeditionis Hispanorum in Angliam vera descriptio Anno D. MDLXXXVIII." This series of excellent maps, showing vividly the Armada's progress through the English Channel, was one of the most ambitious attempts of all contemporary engravers. Published in 1589, these plates made from drawings by Robert Adams, Queen Elizabeth's surveyor, are neat and precise in character, conventional in treatment as regards the ships themselves, yet in their decorative effect most pleasing. They are now rare, but there is a perfect set in the British Museum. In the year 1739 they were copied and published by John Pine.

Ryther's work shows how splendidly the English mind had already adapted itself to the new demands ; for his skill was at least as great as that of Franz Hogenberg. When it was decided to bring out an English version of Wagenaer's atlas, Ryther, together with Hondius (as already mentioned), and Remigius Hogenberg, engraved some of the maps. The title-page, however, was done on the plate by Theodore de Bry, about whom we shall speak presently. This altogether fascinating volume is very much to be coveted by any collector of nautical prints, not merely for its historical and practical interest, but because of its decorative attraction. The ornamented title-page sets forth clearly its scope in the following words :

" The Mariners Mirrour wherein may playnly be seen the courses, heights, distances, depths, soundings, flouds and ebs, risings of lands, rocks, sands and shoalds, with the marks for th' entrings of the Harbouroughs, Havens and Ports of the greatest part of Europe : their seueral traficks and commodities : Together wth the Rules and instrumēts of Navigation First made and set fourth in diuers exact Sea-Charts, by that famous Nauigator Luke Wagenar of Enchuisen And now fitted with necessarie additions for the use of Englishmen by Anthony Ashley."

The first known map of the British Isles was that drawn before 150 A.D., which is reproduced in the 1478 edition of Ptolemy's *Cosmographia* printed at Rome ; but this forms part of a " tabula " showing Europe. Actually the first printed map of England *alone* is that which was drawn by Humphrey Lhuyd and printed at Antwerp in the year 1573.* The earliest known printed map showing any part of America is one of the world, wherein can be seen very crudely the West Indies and part of the American coast. The date is 1506 and it is by Joannes Matheus Contarenus (whose name appears otherwise unknown) and Franciscus Rosellus of Florence, who was working as late as 1532. No collector can ever

---

* In the Additamentum of Ortelius' Atlas, embellished with five ships.

hope to obtain this most rare item. But a unique copy has recently been added to the British Museum, and when we remember that the first voyage of Columbus westward was in only 1492, this new acquisition is quite remarkable.

England was a century behind the Continent in line-engraving, and from 1550 until 1640 the real home of the industry was at Antwerp, which by its geographical position and relation to the sea was the great commercial centre of Western Europe. The word " industry " is used advisedly, since a large number of anonymous hack engravers were employed by the printsellers to produce what correspond to our modern anonymous half-tone engravings. Some Englishmen, such as Benjamin Wright, thus found employment abroad and latterly he widened his knowledge by travel. It is characteristic of the influence made by sixteenth-century ocean voyages and sea-fights that he was called upon to do maps of such places as Java, Sumatra, Madagascar. In 1600 he did one of the Pacific, also of Mexico, Central America and the Caribbean dated 1601. He further included within his work the Atlantic, with coasts of New France, Labrador, Greenland, and Western Europe together with a very spirited scene of whaling.

It was the religious troubles on the Continent which had something to do with the encouragement of engraving and the spread of maritime interest. By the middle of the sixteenth century Lutheranism had been accepted by most of the North German states, and Franz Hogenberg had left the Low Countries for Protestant Cologne during the height of Alva's persecution. So, also, a Fleming named Theodore or Dirck de Bry, who had been born at Liège in 1528, left his home about 1560 and settled at Strassburg, where for nearly thirty years he carried on his avocation as a goldsmith and ornamental engraver. But very late in his life there came a great crisis, which exemplifies how strangely a single event can set going tremendous effects. History is full of these instances, as every one who looks back to July 1914 well realizes.

Now in 1586 Sir Philip Sidney, who had been sent by Elizabeth to the Netherlands, was mortally wounded and his body was brought back to England. In the following year a volume was to be published by Thomas Lant, relating the order of the obsequies, entitled *Sequitur celebritas et pompa funeris*. De Bry in the meanwhile came over to England and was entrusted with the task of engraving thirty plates for this work. It is now very rare, but there is a copy in the British Museum. To us it is of especial fascination, since it contains a really vivid and accurate print of *The Black Pynnes*, which brought Sir Philip's body across the North Sea. Prints of pinnaces are not many, yet there are so frequent references to this type of craft that we are thankful to de Bry for his commemoration. In comparison with the contemporary galleon she was as the light-cruiser of to-day is to the battleship. And in the engraving under consideration we have a well-drawn pinnace with her waist-cloths and netting rigged, her shields and brave Tudor flags.

In 1588 de Bry paid his second visit to England and signed his plates for the above-mentioned *Mariners' Mirror*, which Sir Anthony Ashley, Clerk of the Privy Council, had translated from Wagenaer, with additions. This was the momentous year of the Armada, when the sea-fever in England was at its height, and de Bry was going about amid a fervour of adventure and discovery. But for the present he was anxious to obtain permission to engrave the drawings made by Jacques Le Moyne, who had accompanied the French leader Laudonnière on his ill-fated efforts to found a Huguenot colony in Florida during 1563–1565. Le Moyne had died, de Bry received sanction from the widow, but now came a meeting which prevented these drawings from being engraved until after de Bry's death. For at this stage enters Richard Hakluyt, who six years previously had published his *Divers Voyages touching the Discovery of America*, and was now about to give the world in 1589 his great classic, *Principall Navigations, Voiages, and Discoveries of the English Nation*. This eager geographer and historian, full of belief in the future of seafaring and transoceanic colonization, persuaded de Bry to postpone the Florida engravings and, instead, begin the illustrating of a grand series of voyages and travels. De Bry made the great decision which was to alter his own life and send others longing to travel and colonize.

Hakluyt introduced him to John White, a painter, who had been to Virginia in that expedition sent out by Sir Walter Raleigh led by Sir Richard Grenville. In 1588 T. Hariot had published in England *A briefe and true report of the new found land of Virginia*, and now de Bry decided to make a beginning of Hakluyt's idea. At the age of sixty, when most men think of retiring, de Bry went back to the Continent, established himself in a workshop at Frankfort, and with tremendous enthusiasm began to produce a vast series of plates. The first to appear were two years later, when he brought out the Frankfort edition of Hariot's book, illustrated after Hariot's designs, and for the rest of his life (that is to say during the next ten years) he proceeded to make his own name famous by his prodigious and splendid artistic achievements.

Theodore de Bry was one of the most skilful line-engravers of the whole sixteenth century. He interpreted on copper the zeal for ships, the glory of sea travel, and the romance of exploration as few have ever done. What Hakluyt achieved by writing and lecturing de Bry brought about by his prints. As actual designer on metal, as bookseller and printseller, this exiled Fleming carried on a considerable business. His technique shows a neat style with meticulous care for detail, and for this reason we are able to regard ships and boats and crews as they appeared to Elizabethan Europe.

In 1590 he began his celebrated *Collectiones Peregrinationum in Indiam Occidentalem*, of which the undertaking was so vast that only seven parts appeared during his lifetime ; but the work was carried to completion in 1634 by his widow, his two sons Jan Theodore and Jan Israel, and his two sons-in-law, Matthew Merian and William Fitzer. Theodore de Bry worked almost wholly with the graver, and his plates are usually marked " T.B." or with a cypher. Whilst it is possible sometimes to pick up loose an occasional de Bry engraving for a pound or two, yet it must be remembered that a complete series in Latin, German, or French fetches high prices. Seven years ago his *Voyages to America* (in Latin), 11 parts ; *Voyages to America* (in German), 14 parts ; *Voyages to the East Indies* (in Latin), 11 parts ; *Voyages to the East Indies* (in German), 13 parts—a total of 49 volumes—realized the sum of £315.

I would first draw attention to de Bry's maps, of which two are here given. The first was printed in 1594 and shows the amount of geographical information that was known to the world a hundred years after Columbus had first brought his little squadron into West Indian waters ; and the extent of cartographical knowledge at the eve of Drake's departure for the Caribbean on what was to be his final expedition. For information de Bry was indebted to the data obtained from all those authors who had written on the subject during the past century, but especially to Jeremy Benzon. This interesting map is therefore a graphic synthesis of all the available knowledge. It is even more than that : for there is a running commentary alongside the localities notable for their events connected with the early navigators, and it will well repay the reader to spend an hour with his magnifying glass going from island to island. Here are shown, with general surprising accuracy, the islands and the mainland of North and South and Central America. The illuminative Latin descriptions, the three-masted ships of the period, the whales and sea-monsters make this map of the West Indies a positive delight.

The next map by the same engraver represents the Western Hemisphere as it was known and being studied in 1596. It is embellished with figures of the four great explorers, Columbus, Vespucius, Magellan, and Drake. In the top left-hand corner we have a sketch of what is probably meant to be either the caravel *Pinta* or *Nina* which accompanied the *Santa Maria* on the initial voyage. Rigged with square sails on the foremast, with a lateen on each of the other two masts, the smaller type of ship so typical of the Mediterranean is truthfully indicated by one who evidently took infinite pains to get his facts as accurate as might be possible. The topsails shown in the big ship off the south-east coast of South America are in accordance with our nautical knowledge of such craft.

We next come to a series of adventures in different seas, which at once show de Bry's skill as an artist and some intimate minutiæ of sixteenth-century seafaring that cannot fail to aid us in a reconstruction of the past. Now, by way of preface, let it be said that one of the best travel accounts of the age has been left to us by a man named Hans Stade, who during the period 1547 to 1555 made two voyages to Brazil, which had been discovered by Cabral as recently as 1500, and was claimed for the Portuguese, who took possession of the country by virtue of the treaty of Tordesillas between Spain and Portugal confirmed by the Papal Bull of 1506. Stade journeyed by way of Bremen and Holland to Portugal, and at Lisbon joined a ship as gunner, being one of those people who were anxious to see the world. His written account of the Brazil undertaking was first published in 1557, but in 1592 de Bry brought out an illustrated edition. The print here shown is from this series and intended to indicate that, after Stade's arrival at Funchal, Madeira, the ship sailed across to the town of Cape de Gel (the modern Arzila), a little south of the Gibraltar Straits. Cape de Gel was then part of the Barbary coast in the hands of the Moors. The stay here was brief, for trouble arose and the Moors came riding down to the beach, thus compelling the visitors to sail back to Funchal.

Whilst we shall find that some of these de Bry plates are more fanciful than true to the particular incident; whilst, as in the *Nuremberg Chronicle*, the art editor is not above using the same block, for reasons of economy, to illustrate more than one episode; yet that does not invalidate either the artistic merits of the print or its illuminative particulars. For instance, the ships if lacking in proportion are so clear in their architecture and rigging, the fisher-men's boat with their catch hung up in the sun, the rowing boats, the quayside, and the rest are all valuable items.

The next seven prints are taken from Jeremy Benzon's *History of the New World* which de Bry illustrated and published in 1594. Now Benzon was a Milanese who at the age of twenty-two felt the call of the unknown and set out for adventures in the New World. Here he remained fourteen years, then came back to Europe and caused the above history of the New World to be printed. This was so well received by the Old World that it ran through several editions. In the first engraving we are to understand that Benzon, having proceeded from Seville to San Lucar de Barrameda in a small boat, here managed to get a passage aboard a merchant ship in which he sailed to the Grand Canary and thence to Las Palmas *en route* for America. De Bry's difficulty was that he desired to show the reader Seville, yet he had no genuine view at hand (*legitimam picturam ad manum non haberet*), so with perfect candour he warns the reader that he has used an imaginary port which would do for anywhere. None the less there are certain features here represented which are of historical truth and should not be missed.

Notice, for instance, the fisherman's sloop with its foresail and sprit mainsail. This is one of the clearest and earliest instances of the fore-and-aft rig revealed by an engraver. She is of the same family as many of the modern Dutch craft not quite banished by steam and motors, and her small cabin is easily observed. Two forms of fishing are discernable : the seine and the dip-net. Such sidelights will be found not less entertaining than the designs of the ocean-going ships, the wharf, and the field-guns in the fortifications, such as might be seen in many a sixteenth-century harbour.

After a fortnight's voyage running before the north-east trades, Benzon's ship found herself among seabirds and flying fish. The latter would be a source of keen interest to untravelled Europeans, so de Bry has shown the fish in plenty as they fall on deck. It is true that the engraver uses this plate elsewhere, but what matter ? He was anxious to give his public full dramatic value, and this was one of his most painstaking efforts. In looking through his achievements it becomes quite obvious that either in Flanders or England de Bry had made very careful studies of one particular three-masted contemporary ocean-going ship. There is no fake about this, and he certainly had an eye for a sailing craft. In this particular print, for example, he has taken great trouble to show the parrels by which the yards were kept close to the masts. The manner of stowing the two anchors on the starboard side, with the flukes secured by ropes ; the seamen going out along the bowsprit towards the sprit-sail ; the military roundtop at the main with its ready-for-use supply of darts ; the bonnet which could be unlaced from the foot of the sails (and thus make the equivalent of a reef being taken in), all such items cannot be passed over lightly. They have been shown deliberately by one who understood the way of a ship on the sea.

When in the year 1498 Columbus set forth on his third historic

(Page 52)

OLANDO AT VERAGUA. *Engraved by*
THEODORE DE BRY, 1594.

(Page 53)

PIZARRO AND ALMAGRO MAKE A SOLEMN OATH.
Engraved by THEODORE DE BRY, 1596.

PLATE 10

(Page 54)

THE "AMSTERDAM" ATTACKED BY EAST INDIANS. *Engraved by the* DE BRYS *in* 1601.

(Page 56)

THE INCIDENTS OFF COCHIN.
Engraved by the DE BRYS, 1601.

PLATE 11

(Page 57)

BURIAL OF ADMIRAL JACOB MAHU.
Engraved by the **DE BRYS, 1602.**

(Page 58)

OFF THE COAST OF FLORIDA.
Engraved by the **DE BRYS, 1609.**

PLATE 12

(Page 60)　　　　BATTLE ON THE ZUYDER ZEE, OCTOBER 11, 1573.
From an engraving by an unknown Dutch artist.

(Page 61)　　　　SPANISH ARMADA IN THE ENGLISH CHANNEL, 1588.
From one of the Visscher engravings.

PLATE 13

(Page 62)

"GOLDEN LION," 550 TONS. *From one of the Visscher engravings.*

(Page 62)

"WHITE BEAR," BUILT 1564. *From one of the Visscher engravings*

PLATE 14

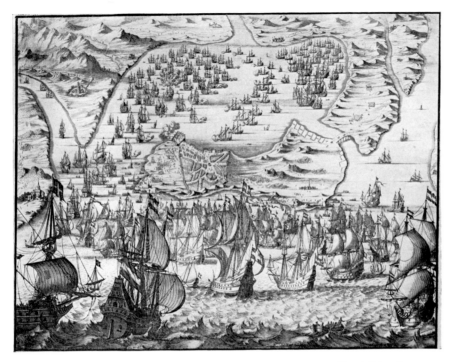

(Page 63)

CAPTURE OF CADIZ, 1596. *From an early Dutch line engraving.*

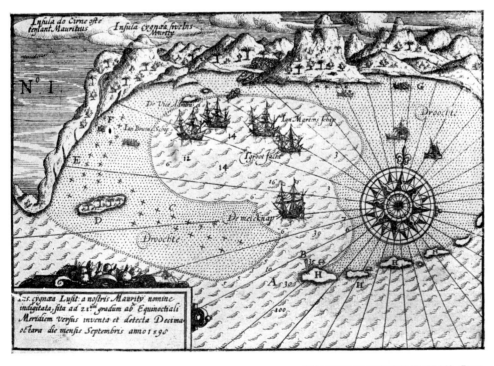

(Page 64)

MAURITIUS HARBOUR PLAN. *From the contemporary engraving of 1600.*

PLATE 15

(Page 65)   **CALLAO HARBOUR.** *From the contemporary engraving of* **1619.**

(Page 67)   **ISLE DE RHE INCIDENT, 1626.** *From* **DUCLARO'S** *contemporary engraving.*

PLATE 16

(Page 71)

ADMIRAL TROMP'S LAST FIGHT, 1653.
From the engraving published by Visscher.

PLATE 17

voyage he sailed over the Atlantic and discovered the northern portion of the South American mainland. Entering the Gulf of Paria he reached the island of Cubagua, better known to us as Trinidad, the second largest of our British West Indian islands. Referring for a moment to de Bry's 1594 map of the West Indies, it will be noticed that the engraver has carefully inscribed alongside Cubagua the statement that " in istam insulam delatus est tertia navigatione Columbus." Further westward is the island of Margarita, which Columbus named the Isle of Pearls, for he happened to see Indians fishing for oysters ; and the latter, on examination by the Spaniards, were found to be filled with large single pearls, whereat the voyagers rejoiced greatly. They therefore bartered trifles with the natives, and from now onwards down to the end of Elizabethan endeavour, right through the reign of James I, European adventurers proceeding west could never get rid of the idea that the New World was rich with pearls and wealthy with mines of gold. It took many years of disappointment and bitterness to dispel this suggestion. I have included here de Bry's print relating Columbus' visit. " It was named the Isle of Pearls," says the author, " because of their plenty." The fishermen with their oysters, the native women with their pearls, the divers at work, are all quaintly presented.

Continuing his story of America, Benzon tells how the pearl fishery on Margarita island was exploited by the Spaniards until the natives rebelled against the cruel treatment ; whereupon the Spaniards took severe measures, lashed the Indians' hands together and then hanged them from the yardarm. The plate which here illustrates this ghastly incident is valuable for a totally different interest. De Bry has sought to provide for our enjoyment a ship such as would really satisfy the eye of a critical sailor. Who but a conscientious craftsman would have taken so much trouble over the

OSP—E

shrouds which support the mast? This rigging—six ropes each side for the mainmast, five for the foremast, and four for the mizzen—is shown hooked on to eyebolts. The hawse-holes, the gun-ports, the rudder and tiller at the square stern, the slings for the yards, the sheaves, are all so accurately reproduced that one could make an excellent model therefrom with perfect confidence.

Less accurate is the allegorical plate which some have called " The Dream of Columbus," where he stands on his deck in armour holding the banner of the cross. The unseamanlike conception of the ship with an anchor lying foul of a gun, the ocean dangerous with buxom mermaids and Neptune's chariot, might more fittingly be regarded as the navigator's nightmare. But this lapse is atoned for as we pass on to a further marine adventure. Benzon is here telling us the story which must readily have appealed to de Bry's imagination. Diego di Niquesa, who discovered Darien in 1509, was voyaging in a caravel accompanied by a couple of other sailing ships which were under the command of one named Olando. But during the night a heavy gale piped up which separated Niquesa from the other two vessels. For a hundred miles Olando searched up and down yet could not find him, and those were the days of mutual mistrust, of mutinous crews, of bold but desperate resolutions.

Olando, in order to prevent his men from escaping, took the deliberate course of piling his ships on the beach at Veragua, which will be found marked on the north side of the Panama neck in de Bry's West Indies map already mentioned. Olando then set his men to work building huts and sowing the fields with maize ; but, later on, he repented of his impetuosity in casting away his vessels. He therefore began to build a caravel out of the wrecked timber. The engraving before us is a very beautiful piece of work, which will delight any print collector, but as a story-teller it is not less entertaining. As was the frequent custom of the day, the designer has in one illustration given a composite idea of several events which happened at different stages of time. Thus we see one of the ships being wrecked, the men at work in the fields and on the huts, others recovering with bill-hooks the broken timber, whilst others again are working as shipwrights. Two are busy with a saw, one in using his adze, a fourth is wielding his hammer. Possibly de Bry got his details from some Flemish shipyard, where he sketched the ship in frame, the callipers, the axes, and the fire as they actually stood. But, in any case, this is just the print one is glad to possess if one really desires to have first-hand information about the sixteenth century and its sea-adventurers.

Whilst it needed such a man as de Bry to urge European imagination towards a venture into the New World, there had already been others in addition to Stade, Benzon and the rest who were so ripe with courage and romantic determination that nothing could keep them away from crossing the Atlantic. Such a character was the Spanish Francisco Pizarro, who had first seen military service in Italy under Gonzalvo di Cordova. Pizarro sailed off with that other Spaniard Vasco Nunez de Balboa and, having explored the Panama isthmus, sighted from a mountain the Pacific in September 1513, when " possession " was taken of this ocean in the name of the Spanish king. In the year 1532 Pizarro set off with Almagro for the conquest of Peru. A rough fellow, not lacking in treacherous intent when it suited him, Pizarro managed to take prisoner the Inca king after having persuaded the latter to a rendezvous. Then putting the Inca to death, Pizarro and Almagro sacked Cuzco. Eventually quarrels broke out between the two Spaniards, and in 1541 Pizarro was assassinated by the Almagrists.

The incident which de Bry has given us is an occasion when

Pizarro and Almagro, after one of their disputes, had become reconciled. On coming ashore they had taken a solemn oath on the Sacred Host promising fidelity to each other; whereupon Pizarro sailed from Panama southwards towards Peru. The crew are seen taking off stores and arms to the ship, whilst the two leaders are making their pact that was afterwards to be broken. But not all de Bry's plates deal with America. It is, however, likely that in the next four which follow he had no technical part, and his affectionate regard for ship accuracy seems to be lacking. At any rate these particular specimens did not leave the press until several years after his death.

In the first, which was printed in 1601, the engraving illustrates an important voyage of the Dutch to Java and Sumatra during the years 1595 to 1597. Let it be remembered that the Netherlands, with their contiguity to the sea, had grown to great maritime adility owing to their successful fisheries, especially in regard to the herring, which during the fifteenth century had changed its spawning ground from the Baltic to the North Sea. So valuable had the industry become that in the year 1560, for example, the year's fishing trade in regard to Holland, Zeeland, Friesland and Flanders amounted to £300,000. With this annual wealth, and by this nautical knowledge gained through seafaring in " doggers " and " haring busses," they were able to build ocean-going craft which would carry national ambition into the unknown parts of the globe. The influence of Flemish printers and engravers through books and maps had carried on that impulse which Prince Henry the Navigator had created throughout Europe. At Antwerp and Bruges excellent schools of cartography had grown up as they had in Portugal and Spain : the amazing stories of the East made the Low Countries long to obtain cargoes of the rich goods that were already waiting. Antwerp was still one of the great European marts, and did a considerable trade not merely with London but with Lisbon, and Oriental news was readily passed from merchant to merchant. There was Jan Huygen von Linschoten, a native of Haarlem, who was typical of the inquiring and ambitious Dutchman. He was a keen student of geography at a time when such knowledge was meagre ; but whilst resident in Lisbon, he collected many valuable data concerning the harbours, the configuration, and the trade winds of the East, from those Portuguese who knew all about the Orient and its possibilities. Later on Linschoten himself visited India and sojourned at Goa, but in 1592 he returned to Europe with tales that astonished his fellow-countrymen.

It is true that his valuable book containing maps and priceless Oriental experience was not published till 1596, of which an English translation appeared a couple of years later and had no little influence on the founding of our first East India Company. So important was the book, however, that there were also editions in Latin, French, and German. But already in 1595 an expedition had been fitted out consisting of four ships which were sent from Holland under Cornelis Houtman. These were to find their way to the countries situate the other side of the Cape of Good Hope beyond the Indian Ocean. The print before us enables us to visualize the four vessels, that in the foreground being the *Amsterdam* at the time when, being in despair of doing any trade, they set sail from Bantam and came to four other cities. The incident represented is the occasion when, several boatloads of natives having been allowed to come aboard and inspect the Dutch goods, these East Indians suddenly drew their knives, tried to seize the *Amsterdam*, and killed a dozen of the crew. A desperate encounter then took place and the natives were driven overboard with a loss of over a hundred. In the meanwhile boats from the other three ships came rowing off to assist the Dutchmen.

But the voyage turned out a commercial success, a trade treaty was made with the King of Bantam, and on arriving back home from Java in 1597 this little squadron * had been able to open up the East to Holland and thus make the beginnings of the Dutch East Indian wealth. That, in turn, was to build up a powerful seventeenth-century navy and to enable those splendid Dutch painters to create such wonderful portraits and shipping scenes for future remembrance. In 1598 a fleet of eight ships was dispatched from Amsterdam to Java and the East Indies, and this voyage concluded two years later. In 1601 its eventful experiences were illustrated by the de Brys, and I have included the plate, which is another of those composite affairs giving three scenes in one. The size of the figures to the ship is, of course, out of all proportion, but the engraver wishes to tell the story clearly and dramatically. For in the neighbourhood of Cochin one of the fleet had trouble with her rudder. A man was sent overboard to adjust it, whereupon a shark came and bit off first one of his legs then one of his hands and his arm. The ghastly episode up to the moment when the poor fellow was taken ashore has been carefully reproduced for the benefit of those interested.

Such enterprising expeditions were the outcome of trading companies. In England the oldest was the Hamburg Company, which consisted of English merchants doing commerce with Calais, Holland, Zeeland and the neighbourhood, and had been incorporated as far back as 1296. There was also the Russian Company of the sixteenth century, which had been inaugurated by some English merchants who sent three ships to seek a north-east passage into Asia and the East. Similarly there was the Levant Company, founded in 1581 to trade with the East Mediterranean ; and then

* Only three of the four ships returned, with most of the crews dead or sick ; these three formed part of the eight ships sent out in 1598.

in 1600 came the English East India Company, which actually grew out of the last-mentioned.

In 1602 the de Brys published at Frankfort an illustrated account of De Wert's voyage through the Magellan Straits to the Far East, entitled *Relatio Historica sive vera et genvina consignatio ac Descriptio Illius Navigationis . . ,* to commemorate a certain expedition of five ships sent for the purpose of extending their new Eastern trade. Equipped at the cost of a merchant company, they were not to use the South African route but, after sailing through the Magellan Straits, were to plunder the Spanish settlements of Chili and Peru, and then cross the Pacific Ocean. Primarily these three-masted ships were to be traders, but they were fitted out as men-of-war so as to be capable of fighting wherever necessary with a view to profit. With them went that experienced English navigator William Adams (born 1575, died 1620), a native of the Medway, who also spent the last twenty years of his life in Japan. The print here taken from that voyage shows the expedition at the island of Barva, Cape Verdes, and is another composite effect showing several incidents simultaneously. We are to understand that having in vain bargained for their needs with some Portuguese (seen on a hill to the right), the Dutch burst their way into a deserted house, found a store of maize and carried the food away. But whilst at this anchorage there died the Dutch admiral of the expedition, Jacob Mahu. His coffin is seen being first carried along the deck and then lowered over the ship's side, after having been weighted down with stones. A fanfare of trumpets from each ship and the firing of guns give the final salute.

In 1609 the de Brys published a set of twelve Le Moyne plates illustrating the second voyage of the French to Florida (already mentioned) under Rene de Laudonnière, which was made in 1564, the first having occurred in 1560 under Ribaut ; though it will be recollected that Jacques Cartier, who crossed the Atlantic in 1534 with two small vessels, touched at Newfoundland and discovered New Brunswick, and during his second voyage of 1535–36 discovered also the St. Lawrence, of which he took possession on behalf of the French king. In 1541 he made yet a third voyage. But the print before us (from the second part of de Bry's *American Grands Voyages*) indicates a scene which Ribaut had named Cape Gaul in honour of his country, where to the northward ran a river. This Laudonnière now named the River Dolphin, owing to the number of such creatures being there found. The engraver has shown us the friendly Indians, the two three-masted ships, and a couple of open boats, but it is impossible to identify the place-names as the colony was completely stamped out by de Aviles.

Thus, in short, the print collector who cares to base a section of his hobby on the early adventurers and explorers of the Indies, East and West, will find the de Bry plates both numerous and satisfying. He will be able to visit America, North and South, cross the Pacific, and see the beginnings of European expansion all over the globe. And, as this section gradually swells into a large portfolio, all the romance of living history, and the glamour of geography take on a new attraction. With Columbus he can cruise through the Caribbean, with Cabral sight the coast of Brazil, with Balboa cross the isthmus of Darien, and from the mountain catch sight of the Pacific which Balboa named the Gulf of St. Michael because it was September and Michaelmas Day. With Magellan he can sweep through the harsh Magellan Straits during November into the waters of the ocean which seemed so calm that he named it the Mar Pacifico. In Pizarro's company he can watch the conquest of Peru and see the beginnings of Spanish colonization in South America, the subsequent intermittent trade between Europe and the Pacific, the coming of the English fleets to plunder the Spanish galleons. In Drake's company he can watch the great explorer look across the Panama isthmus to the warm waters of the Southern Sea as Balboa had done previously. With Laudonnière the print enthusiast can reach Florida, or with the Dutch seek the East Indies ; in short, wherever ships had sailed he can indulge his imaginative delight and enjoy the freedom of the seas.

CHAPTER V

PRINTS AND THE RISE OF SEA-POWER

So many all-important deeds in the clash of wills on sea were happening in the late sixteenth and seventeenth centuries that contemporary thought insisted on illustrating by the most expressive manner something of the great emotions which had been aroused. Now there are few, if any, forces which so excite the mental condition of a community as either religious indignation or alien aggression ; but when these two causes unite in one it is certain that the degree of feeling must reach extraordinary heights.

In the Netherlands the spread of Protestantism and the rebellion against super-imposed Spanish rule created an attitude which is difficult to put in words. It was, however, expressed in terms of warfare and afterwards in art. The revolt of many Dutch towns, the activities of the " Beggars of the Sea," and the culminating battle of the Zuyder Zee on October 11–12, 1573, when the Dutch fleet gained a signal victory over the Spaniards, capturing five of the latter's ships as well as their admiral, so influenced the trend of history that we are entitled to see how a contemporary engraver illustrated the crisis.

Plate 13, upper picture, shows the literal clash against the Spanish flagship in the foreground. The usual three-masters with their squaresails and lateen mizzens are engaged in gunnery duels and boarding ; but we see also the Spanish galleys under sail and oars, and—nearer to the Enkhuisen coast—the smaller fore-and-aft Dutch craft running before the wind under sprit-sails. Below the design are five commemorative verses of this national victory, but whoever the artist may have been there are features in this plate which remind one of de Bry's work. The general detailed care, and the body of a man diving from the Spanish flagship's poop will at once strike the memory as at least suggesting a definite school of engraving.

Another of these continental print-makers, one of the well-known Visscher family, has shown similar exultation in the Spanish Armada's defeat, and the next three examples come under this category. In 1580 was born, at Amsterdam, Claes (or Nikolaes) Jansz Visscher, who was both engraver and printseller like his father before him. There was also Cornelis Visscher, another engraver of the same family, who was born in the same city in 1620, and died fifty years later. This extremely able technician had a brother Jan who, among other plates, did a portrait of the Dutch Admiral de Ruyter ; and another brother, Lambert Visscher, engraved Admiral Cornelis Tromp's portrait. Still, the Visscher firm published not merely their own prints but such contemporary work as that of Romeyn de Hooge's Dutch invasion of the Medway and the Battle of La Hogue.

The Visscher engraving of the Armada shows a not very pleasing version of the operations in the Dover Straits. On comparing this with a similar print in the British Museum Print Room one notices that certain alterations have been made by some craftsman. Whilst in the main both examples are identical, yet in the British Museum impression Calais is shown where you see Dover, and Dover is placed where you see Calais. The maintopsail of the big ship in the foreground to the left of the centre has the figure and name of St. Andrew, but the reader will observe that in our impression this is now scarcely traceable. In like fashion the banner with a saint on the foremast has been almost obliterated. But we are very grateful to the C. J. Visscher—there is such confusion as to identities that it is impossible always to get clear the relationship—who engraved so exquisitely the large-scale Elizabethan ships. Both *Golden Lion* and *White Bear* did very good service. The former was a vessel of 550 tons, one of the royal craft, and was with Drake's squadron when in 1587 he carried out that brilliant campaign of singeing the Spaniard's beard. *White Bear* was another of the Crown Navy. This fine, big galleon of 915 tons had been built in 1564 and was four-masted. Who can look at her high-charged decks, her quarter-galleries, the hooks fixed to the yardarms (for injury to the enemy's rigging when boarding), the ship's bell, the royal standard, the green and white Tudor ensign, and the flag of St. George, without realizing that the exploits of Elizabethan seamen become vivid and real to our imaginations ?

This C. J. Visscher, who died in 1660, was responsible for an *Atlas Minor* consisting of 126 maps, published at Amsterdam in 1656. It was a copy of this work, coloured by contemporary hand, which in 1923 fetched £20 in the saleroom. But the student who desires to contemplate the finest of Elizabeth's men-of-war must visit the British Museum and see a contemporary woodcut of *The Ark Royal* in the Print Room. The vessel had been built in 1587 and served as the flagship for Lord Howard of Effingham. This cut is of unique value, but the collector will naturally bear it in mind when looking for authentic representations. Sir William Monson gave her tonnage as 800 and her crew as 400 ; and we know that Elizabeth purchased her from Sir Walter Raleigh for £5,000. Notwithstanding that Tudor figures are not always reliable it would seem that the number of *Ark Royal's* crew was in proper relation to her size ; for I have examined in the above museum an interesting little manuscript memorandum book that once belonged to William Cecil, Lord Burghley (1520—1598), and still contains various notes concerning private and public matters of about the year 1592. He gives a list of the English naval ships, with their stations, tonnage, and personnel for May 20, from which it is evident that vessels of 500 tons carried 220 men and those units of 200 tons carried 100. Seeing that for forty eventful years this great statesman practically controlled England's destiny, he would doubtless be accurately informed.

In the South Kensington Museum will be found a print by John Gallé (1600—1676), which is after an original by John Stradanus (1523—1605), and represents another of these sixteenth-century fighting ships. It is worth examining, for it shows her at sea with her wheeled-carriage guns such as were used ashore, the pilot taking a compass observation of the sun, most of the crew below the nettings in the waist, and the shields outside as early protective armour. But a Dutch line-engraver, in that fashion already mentioned, has contrived at once a harbour plan of Cadiz and a spirited record of the operations of 1596 when Howard was sent with Essex and Raleigh to anticipate Philip, who was reported to be making preparations on a large scale for a fresh attempt on England. This print is reproduced (Plate 15), because it makes so clear the topographical features inside Cadiz with the vast attacking fleet of warships and hired merchantmen. Not without interest is the little vessel slightly to the left of the centre between the two bigger ships : she is one of the earliest two-masted schooners to be shown by any of the engravers. That this small fore-and-after, with her high stern and leeboards, should have been deemed sufficiently war-worthy to accompany a fleet of nearly 140 craft across the Bay of Biscay during the month of June is one of those illuminative items which can often surprise and reward our study of such prints.

There was an English " chart-graver " (as they called such craftsmen at the time) whose name was Thomas Cockson. In 1596 he, too, did a large map illustrating this exploit against Cadiz. It is now exceedingly rare, the only known copy being owned by the Duke of Northumberland. But Cockson presently engraved an equestrian portrait of Howard to celebrate both the defeat of the Armada and the capture of Cadiz. In the background to the left are the invading Spanish fleet, but to the right we have another miniature plan of Cadiz with the Spanish galleons inside, and generally rather similar to the Dutch print.

The next three prints will show how difficult it was for such artists to throw off the chart habit ; on the other hand, the convention served its purposes, and we cannot but admire clarity of design as well as the skill in producing a pleasing subject. Consider this copper-plate plan of Mauritius first. The aim was twofold : the recording of an achievement, and the presentation of sailing directions for those who would require to find their way in to the appropriate anchorage. The soundings, the landmarks of palm trees and mountains, the stream where freshwater could be obtained, the secret position where several articles were left behind for other venturers, and the islets whereon giant tortoises existed, are all set forth in such a manner that the least expert pilot could find sketched just the very guidance required for the safety and welfare of his ship. Nothing could be plainer. Thus the letter A shows the entrance from seaward, B begins the harbour, where palm trees act as the starboard-hand mark. Similarly C denotes the shallows which dry right out, D is an islet, E a saltwater creek, F a freshwater creek, G the place where the articles were hidden, and H the string of islets with the tortoises.

Mauritius had been discovered and held by the Portuguese in 1505 till the Dutch in 1598 arrived and took possession. The former had called the island Ilha de Cerné, but the Hollanders now changed the name in honour of Maurice, Prince of Orange (1567–1625), who so distinguished himself in the war against Spain. Inside the harbour are visible some of the Dutch vessels, for this is the same voyage of eight Dutch ships mentioned in the previous chapter that left Amsterdam in 1598. The line engraving has, however, been taken from the first edition of the original journal printed in Amsterdam by Cornelis Claez apt Water in the year 1600. This rare and valuable book, gilt-edged and handsomely bound, was formerly in the celebrated Huth collection. It consists of only forty-three pages and there should be eighteen plates, which are practically the same as in de Bry's edition of 1601. Some of the blocks seem to have been reversed, and they differ in such details as the names of ships or in not having the key-numbers corresponding to the descriptions of the text.

This *Journael ofte Dagh-register*, written by Jacob Cornelis Neck, the admiral of the expedition, left the Texel on May 1, rounded the Cape of Good Hope, and on September 18, 1598, reached Mauritius. Four ships arrived back in Holland by July of the following year, but the other four went on from Java to the Moluccas and did not reach home till 1600.

But in the bird's-eye view of Callao we observe a somewhat similar manner of providing such a picture-plan as would be of practical value to other seafarers. This line-engraving is taken from another of those published Dutch journals, or diaries, which possessed almost the value of a ship's log. Peru's principal port, extending along two miles of bay between sea and Andes, is presented as it appeared on July 20, 1615. For we have before us the entertaining account of George Spilbergen's voyage with six ships round the world by the Magellan Straits, across the Pacific to the East Indies, where four of the vessels were left behind to carry on trade. This circumnavigation was just one of those new trading ventures which followed logically on the newly-found sea-routes ; and, like astute business men which the Dutch always have been, the merchants were anxious to profit by opening up new markets. It was thus that they were rising gradually and confidently towards that sea-power which must presently clash with English aspirations afloat to bring about the inevitable Anglo-Dutch wars.

The title of this vellum-bound book is *Speculum Orientalis Occidentalisque Indiæ Navigationum*, published in 1619. This rare work contains at the beginning a double-page map of the world indicating Spilbergen's track ; but, having regard to the date, it is not without interest to observe in North America, " The bay wher Hitson did winter," marked in English. Henry Hudson had discovered this Hudson Bay only on his last voyage, and he had been dead just eight years when the *Speculum* was issued. There is no actual mention of Virginia, but Charlesfort (where the young English colony was struggling on the banks of the James river) and Croatan Sound (the scene of the unlucky Raleigh colony attempted at Roanoke Island) are shown. Even if geographical accuracy was not strictly possible, this map proves that the cartographer and engraver were not unaware of the discoveries which had within recent years been made.

The journal begins with the entry : " Eighth of August in the year 1614," when they set sail from the Texel. " May God direct our journey well. Amen." The book contains a separate pictorial plan of the Magellan Straits, embellished with ships and compass card, all very quaint but forming just one of the planks in the platform of knowledge necessary to any who should come after. In the Callao engraving the incident is the arrival of Spilbergen's squadron at the port, only to find many fine Spanish

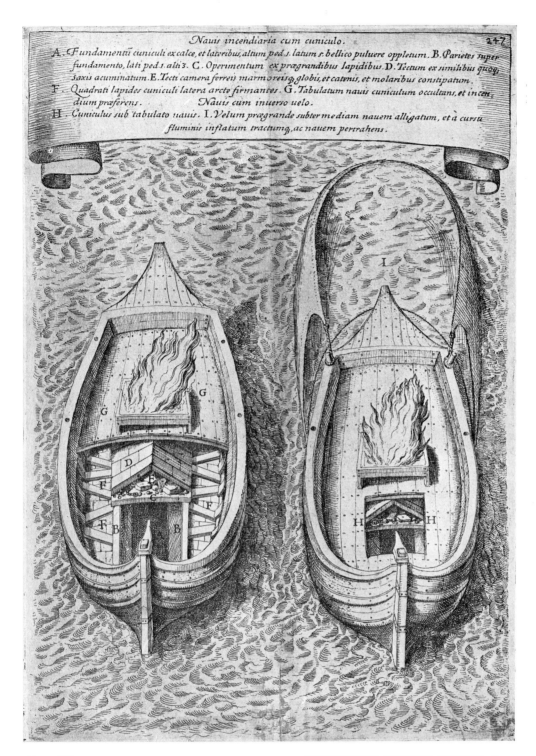

Nauis incendiaria cum cuniculo. 247

A. *Fundamentū cuniculi ex calce, et lateribus, altum ped.1. latum 5. bellico puluere oppletum.* B. *Parietes super fundamento, lati ped.1. alti 3.* C. *Operimentum ex prægrandibus lapidibus.* D. *Tectum ex similibus quoq́, saxis acuminatum.* E. *Tecti camera ferreis marmoreisq́, globis, et catenis, et molaribus constipatum.* F. *Quadrati lapides cuniculi latera arcte firmantes.* G. *Tabulatum nauis cuniculum occultans, et incen-dium præferens.* *Nauis cum inuerso uelo.* H. *Cuniculus sub tabulato nauis.* I. *Velum prægrande subter mediam nauem alligatum, et à cursu fluminis inflatum tractumq́, ac nauem pertrahens.*

(Page 72)   SEVENTEENTH CENTURY FIRESHIP. *From a contemporary print.*

                                                           PLATE 18

(Page 73)   MEDITERRANEAN NAVAL BASE. *From the etching by* STEFANO DELLA BELLA (1610–1664).

(Page 73)   MEDITERRANEAN NAVAL BASE. *From the etching by* STEFANO DELLA BELLA (1610–1664).

PLATE 19

(Page 76)   **DUTCH WARSHIPS AT SEA.** *From the etching by* **R. NOOMS** (*or* **ZEEMAN**). *Published in* **1675.**

(Page 76)   **DUTCH WARSHIPS IN HARBOUR.** *From the etching by* **R. NOOMS** (*or* **ZEEMAN**). *Published in* **1675.**

PLATE 20

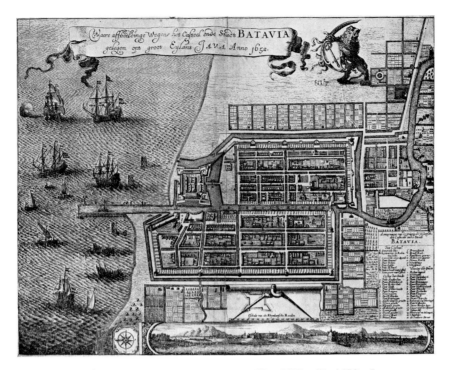

(Page 77)   BATAVIA, JAVA, IN 1652. *From a con-*
temporary Dutch line engraving.

(Page 77)   ENTRANCE TO FLUSHING, 1660. *From a*
contemporary Dutch line engraving.

PLATE 21

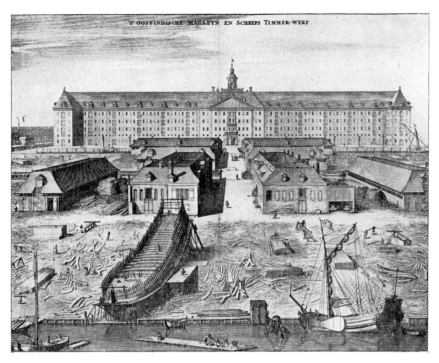

(Page 78)   **AMSTERDAM DOCKYARD FOR EAST INDIAMEN.** *From the contemporary engraving by* **JOSEPH MULDER.**

(Page 78)   **THE BURNT EAST INDIAMAN.** *From a Dutch engraving of about* 1700.

PLATE 22

MAN WITH A ROCKET. *From the mezzotint by* CORNELIS DUSART. *about* 1690.

PLATE 23

THE WAR OF THE SPANISH SUCCESSION.
Dutch line engraving about 1705.

PLATE 24

(Page 82)

To the Rt Honble. the *Principal* OFFICERS and   *COMMISSIONERS* of his MAJ.TIES *NAVY*
This *PLATE* is most   humbly *Inscrib'd*

Baston delin.   *J. Sartor sculp.*

(Page 83)   **ENGLISH SQUADRON BEATING TO WINDWARD.**
Engraved by **J. SARTOR** *after* **THOMAS BASTON.**

PLATE 25

ships already lying there at anchor, and the colony sufficiently established ashore with its church and public buildings.

By the same bird's-eye method did the French engravers succeed in providing at once immortality for an event and an illustrated plan with topographical details. The line-engraving of the Isle de Rhé was the work of a craftsman named Duclaro employed by Melchior Tavernier, himself an engraver and " marchand d'estampes," who was born at Antwerp in 1594 and died in Paris during 1641, where for some time he was copper-plate printer to the King of France. Isle de Rhé is that island, eighteen miles long, separated from the west coast of France by a two-mile passage opposite La Rochelle, and one recalls by this illustration those unhappy religious divisions which became so marked during the seventeenth century. For this corner was a Huguenot stronghold when in 1626 Charles I had sent a naval expedition under Admiral Pennington to aid Richelieu against the French Protestants. The English seamen, however, presented a statement to Pennington refusing to act against a cause with which they shared great sympathy. Weighing anchor, they bore away for England, but before they could reach an English harbour they were ordered into Dieppe, where, on arrival, the crews deserted their ships. This " Pennington affair " caused no little sensation at home, but it remains historic as having been the first occasion when a mutiny ever took place in the English fleet, as apart from trouble in single ships. The view is taken looking south, and the cherub's head is the conventional way of showing the direction of the wind, which in this case was blowing from the south-west. La Rochelle, with its fort, its houses and surrounding fields, is indicated at the top left-hand corner.

In France the earliest line-engravers had come into being long after Germany, the Netherlands, and Italy had become expert ;

OSP—F

but by the latter part of the sixteenth century the art was struggling through its infancy. Such men as Tavernier brought into France from Antwerp some of the technical ability and zeal for what was presently to be so accomplished a French achievement. In England by the first years of the seventeenth century the print-seller had become a familiar figure, and cultured people were already exhibiting a genuine interest, especially in the maps of Ortelius, Mercator, Hondius and others. Whilst the chief demand was confined to portraits of eminent persons, and to such embellishments as the booksellers ordered, there was sufficient enthusiasm to require in 1624 the final editions of Ortelius' atlas, which had first appeared in 1570; for the Elizabethan sea impulse was still far from dead, Virginia and India were very much in the public mind, Captain John Smith had just been trying by his printed books and personal propaganda to make his countrymen think in colonial channels, and many who had never been outside their own townships now were about to cross the ocean. With the departure of the *Mayflower* in 1620, soon to be followed by many other ships, the time had thus arrived when printed facts and illustrative information concerning distant lands were very much required by merchant adventurers, intending emigrants, and aristocratic leaders with capital to invest.

The Civil War and the unsettled condition of internal politics had a retarding effect on our national school of engravers. It was thus that in this period the centre of progress passed from Flanders to France, though William Faithorne the elder (1616—1691) was able to uphold English portrait engraving in a manner comparable with the ablest efforts of the French. Under the English Charles II the Greenwich Royal Observatory and the *Nautical Almanac* had been founded, navigation was becoming a more advanced art, but the first English charts to be printed (as distinct from adaptations after the Dutch) did not come until there was published G. Collins's *Great Britain's Coasting Pilot*, during the year 1693.

With the gradual reliance on charts, perfected from data brought home by the voyages of Dampier and many another, there departed in time those globes which had once been so popular among navigators. The first globes ever to be made were for astronomical purposes and ascribed to Atlas of Libya; hence, in the development of things, the god who was reputed to sustain on his shoulders the world gave his name to a collection of maps. Strabo and Ptolemy knew all about the construction of globes, and during the Middle Ages celestial spheres in metal were manufactured by those able navigators the Arabs; but in 1492 (the year when Columbus started on his first West Indian voyage) Martin Behaim the German cosmographer, who had been to sea as far south as the River Congo, made at Nuremberg his famous terrestrial globe which measured twenty-one inches in diameter. Other globes engraved on copper followed, and some, such as by Johann Schöner in 1523, showed the track of Magellan.

The first English globes, terrestrial and celestial, were drawn by Emery Molyneux of Lambeth and issued in 1592. Jodocus Hondius, too, made both types and of a size larger than any previously seen. But the pioneer in English navigation was that eminent mathematician Edward Wright, inventor of the true method of projection, who in 1599 published his book, *Certaine Errors in Navigation*. He complained of the proportions of the existing charts, which showed the distances between places wrongly, and advocated Great Circle sailing, so familiar to the navigators of to-day. Wright was acquainted with Hondius and even lent the latter some of his confidential cartographical material, of which the foreigner seems to have made dishonourable use. The first to introduce globes and maps into the common schools was Richard

Hakluyt ; but large globes were made by William Johnson Blaeu, a Dutchman, from whose book Richard Hynmers in 1625 published a translation entitled *The Sea Mirrour*.

Mention must be made of two seventeenth-century English engravers, who are especially known for having reproduced an early map of Old Virginia and New Virginia respectively. Of these we may class Robert Vaughan, who was working by 1622, as a mere hack ; yet William Hole first appears in 1607. Both contributed a number of portraits and whatever fell to them. But a more talented employee of the booksellers was John Payne, who was born in 1620 and learned his work from the Van de Passe family. Although he was lazy, dissipated, and died in want before reaching his twenty-ninth birthday, he has made posterity his debtor by providing one of the finest prints of a ship which ever came out of that century. This is the well-known line-engraving entitled " The True Portraicture of His Maties Royall Ship the *Soveraigne* of the Seas." It is of exceptional size, being done on two plates, which when joined together measured 3 ft. long and 2 ft. 2 in. high. She was, of course, a wonderful vessel of over 1,600 tons, and the largest which English builders had ever built, the envy of both France and the United Provinces. By means of the consummate care and studied detail we are given every possible knowledge as to her external decoration, rigging, running-gear, sails, and flags. This print has been frequently reproduced, and has enabled more than one perfect model to be built up. Nor could we ever expect to find a more illuminative document.

Two instances may be mentioned of the way in which Dutch families continued to keep with themselves the arts of engraving, drawing, painting, and etching. Of the Parcelles family Jan (who was born in Ghent during 1597, worked at Harlem from 1622 until 1680 and died soon afterwards) was both painter and etcher, his scope including such subjects as shipping off the Dutch coast in gales and calms. His son Julius, born in 1628, carried on his father's technique in a manner almost identical. So, too, Romeyn de Hooge, that great genius of engraving, who ably commemorated the rise of Netherlandish sea-power and has made some of the Anglo-Dutch war incidents so vivid, came of an artistic family, his uncle being the great Pieter de Hooge, the painter of quiet interiors and sunlit courtyards. The collector may have to pay as much as £15 for Romeyn's prints, but some of them are rich with life and delicate treatment.

The Visscher print here selected celebrates that last sea-fight between Admiral Tromp against the English at the end of the First Dutch war, on July 31, 1653. After some bitter engagements and a temporary lull, whilst Tromp was refitting his ships and Monck was blockading him, Tromp managed to escape out of the Maas, but on July 29 the English admiral with 106 vessels sighted the enemy off the Texel, who succeeded the following day in joining hands with de Witt. The battle began off Katwijk, and the Dutch coastline has been touched in by the artist. Although Monck found himself confronted by a superior force, the heavier guns of the English fleet were doing terrible damage. And then Tromp was robbed of victory when a musket-ball pierced his heart; he fell dead on the quarter-deck. One by one his units became disheartened and fled home pursued by Monck. Nightfall enabled some to make for their Dutch ports, but twenty-six of them had been burnt, six had been sunk, and nearly five thousand Hollanders had been killed. When in the following spring peace was signed, the terms included an acknowledgment of the claim to a salute of the English flag by the Dutch when in English waters. The artist has caught something of the exciting spirit which marked Tromp's final battle, so that the student will note with interest how admirably and with

what accuracy the engraver has drawn the sterns and broadsides
of these sailing ships. The inset of Tromp himself is a fine bit of
characterization.

Now during this battle the Dutch employed the use of fire-
ships as part of their tactics, and with success : for, having
obtained the weather-gage, they were able thus to set three of our
vessels—the *Oak, Hunter,* and *Triumph*—in flames. The pro-
cedure was, of course, not original and had been adopted with happy
results by the English when the latter on the night of July 28, 1588,
sent eight vessels filled with powder, pitch and brimstone among
the anchored Armada, causing the Spaniards to cut and run. The
next engraving by a contemporary will afford a clear understanding
of these dreaded vessels, which were usually older craft of little
value. The lines of the hull show her to be Dutch, and for our
convenience the after deck has been cut away. After having been
filled with gunpowder, stone, ball, iron and chain below deck, with
a fire burning wildly amidships, the dreaded thing was cast adrift
down to leeward. In order that she might keep her course, stern
first, a big sail (such as an old topsail) was secured at the bows in
a way so that the foot came right below the hull. This would, of
course, act as a drogue and prevent her from yawing about. We
can well imagine the panic which a few of these would create amid
a fleet of sail, and wood, and inflammable rigging.

We come now to examine some of the marine etchings belonging
to this period. This art, descended from the Mediæval armourers,
did not express itself on the printed paper until the beginning of
the sixteenth century, when Urs Graf dated his work, or Daniel
Hopfer, the Augsberg armourer, produced his etched prints.
Quite possibly the Fugger family of Augsberg merchant princes,
who by silver mining and money-lending and speculative trading
all over Europe were to become so enriched, gave encouragement

to Hopfer and others. Dürer, of course, we know soon followed in this young art, Nuremberg contributing several landscape artists who expressed themselves by this method.

About 1520 Lucas van Leyden in the Netherlands etched a few plates ; both Pieter Breughel the elder and Jan Breughel the elder used the same process for landscapes. The earliest Italian etchings synchronize with Lucas van Leyden's, and in France about the same time, or a little later, was Jacques Androuet Ducerceau, who interpreted architecture. It was during the seventeenth century that etching reached its perfection, copper and even steel being used, just as contemporary engravers were working sometimes on brass. But the sixteenth- and early seventeenth-century etchers are more accurately described as engravers, who used the acid to reinforce the already drawn lines cut on the plate with the graver through a hard etching-ground.

Now the first part of this seventeenth century is especially notable for three great technicians of the needle : Jacques Callot (who during the period 1592 to 1635 lived in Nancy, Rome, Florence, and Brussels), Stefano della Bella (who passed the years 1610 to 1664 in Florence, Rome and Paris), and Wenceslaus Hollar (who lived from 1607 to 1677 in Prague, Frankfort, Antwerp and London). The two charming etchings here seen will show the reader how delicate was della Bella's work. In these prints we have the naval energy and customs at some Mediterranean base, with its galleys (not yet dismissed from service even in the middle of that century), the ships-of-the-line, dockyard, and figures.

Della Bella was born at Florence and died there. The son of a goldsmith, he readily enough adapted the work for reproduction, and received his training from the same master who taught Callot. From daily ordinary life as he saw it, from history too, della Bella obtained his many subjects ; but there are in his expression a fantasy, a brilliant execution, and the true taste of an artist. No wonder, then, that Richelieu employed him. But in spite of the considerable genius and fertility of invention which these etchings unquestionably exhibit, they do not fetch high prices to-day. The fact is that such artists were badly remunerated, they were compelled to make a prolific output, and they frequently died in want. Della Bella left behind about fifteen hundred etchings, but of marine subjects there are very few.

Wenceslaus Hollar is an excellent instance of having lived a full life and dying with an empty purse. The son of a lawyer, he was born at Prague, and as a schoolboy used to love drawing maps. From Prague he went to Frankfort where he learned to etch, afterwards working at Strassburg and Cologne. In the latter he became acquainted with Thomas Howard, Earl of Arundel (on an embassy to Ferdinand II), who was a famous art collector. Therefore, in 1636 the noble earl brought Hollar with him on the return to England, and for the next few years we find this foreign artist etching plates after the masterpieces in the Arundel collection and doing work for the London printsellers. In 1639 he was made drawing master in the Royal household, and after a period spent in Antwerp he returned to England in 1652.

Hollar was one of the most productive of all the craftsmen at that time working in England. Primarily an etcher but also an engraver, he made at least three thousand items, and it is from these that ample knowledge is obtained in regard to seventeenth-century London, the Thames, topography and architecture in general, historical scenes, ships, and costumes. As to the latter, his *Ornamentus Muliebris Anglicanus* is a classic containing costumes of the Englishwomen of his time. But he comes into our purview because in 1668 Lord Henry Howard was sent to Tangiers, which had been six years previously ceded to England as part of the dowry of

Catherine of Braganza, wife of our Charles II ; and at the Crown's expense Hollar accompanied Howard to make sketches of the African port. These sketches are still preserved in the British Museum, and seventeen plates he made from them showing Tangiers shipping and buildings.

After spending over a year on this job (" etshd in Copper," as he himself inscribed), he received the sum of £100 and set out for England, his ship being attacked on the way by Algerine pirates. He narrowly escaped being taken prisoner and lived to etch a plate of this exciting incident, which was included in Ogilby's *Africa*. But in his views of ships, great and small, sailing below London Bridge ; in his 1640 " View of the Spanish, Dutch and English Fleets off Deal," we have plenty of evidence that he understood how to do maritime subjects. Unfortunately he was ill-rewarded, although he was kept busily employed by the booksellers etching numerous plates. For this he was given twelvepence an hour plus lodging in a printseller's house, and he died in dire poverty at the age of seventy. Thus does the world recognize a great craftsman.

One word of warning must be made. Years after his death the printsellers published in large numbers indifferent impressions from his plates. These are still to be had at less than £10 each, but even the best Hollar items can be obtained at not more than twice that price. And since it is assumed that the collector's aim should be quality rather than quantity, it is important to be on one's guard and avoid the weak pulls.

Another really excellent etcher was Renier (or Remigius) Nooms, commonly known as Zeeman. His work embraces architecture as well as shipping, and to the latter he brought the same faithful technique essential to the former. Nooms was resident at Amsterdam and his period is slightly vague, but it is within the dates 1612—1675. Among his marine subjects you will find naval fights of 1673 ; Dutch herring-fleets, shipping and ports. But especially are we indebted to a series of twelve prints which were published in Amsterdam by C. Allard and in London by Arthur Tooker, the latter edition being dedicated to Samuel Pepys. The date is 1675 and Nooms was their actual designer. Their value is not merely because they are artistic but that they are nautically authentic. The most critical eye of the seaman can look at Nooms' etchings with unspoiled pleasure. Wandering about the quays and ship-yards of Amsterdam, sketching the men at work constructing and repairing, painting and careening, Nooms gathered his first-hand material and executed his task as could be done only by one who loved and understood ships. In the couple of reproductions the reader will observe some of the Dutch warships at sea and moored in harbour, where hands are busy on the rigging, setting up the yards and generally refitting. So reliable and altogether satisfying are these Nooms, that they make most desirable items in any collection. In the Pepysian Library of Magdalene College, Cambridge, such Nooms etchings will be found bound up at the end of Sir Anthony Deane's *Doctrine of Naval Architecture*. If it is true that Nooms for a time worked with the elder Van de Velde, we can perfectly understand whence he derived some of his ability.

But when we think of all the marine activity which was going on in Dutch ports with the arrival and departure of herring fleets, high-sterned East Indiamen, gilded and carved men-of-war, majestic yachts, and every inhabitant of the Netherlands so keenly affected by the wealth of the sea, can we wonder that such engravers or painters as Justus Danckerts or Jan van de Capelle, or Ludolf Backhuysen, or the Van de Veldes and many another were encouraged to set down every possible aspect of seafaring ? As showing, however, the class of work which was being done by way of book illustration one may call attention to the line-engraving of Batavia, Java, as it appeared in 1652. This is another of those combined illustration-plans giving a bird's-eye view of the port. The topographical features have been drawn to scale, and the roadstead is shown with Dutch three-masters, fore-and-aft sloops, and a native proa. The beacons at the seaward end mark the entrance into the " Groote " river which flows through the town. There is to be bought a well-known print which also represents this port as if seen from the sky, with the canals and buildings all arranged in Dutch-like neatness, but this view is taken looking from the roadstead.

Similar in treatment is the Dutch line-engraving showing the way into Flushing. The date is 1660, but the port has not altered very much in over two and a half centuries. The view of the spires, the churches, and public buildings is extraordinarily like that which the mariner sees to-day as he comes up the Wielingen Channel from the southward and crosses the strong tide of the West Scheldt. Even the windmills are there still, and where the engraver has marked with the figure 7 a " mast craen " for stepping the masts of the old sailing ships, there rises in our modern time a tall steel gantry used in the construction of steamers. Thus the continuity of the marine instinct goes on, with the least interruption by political crises. This particular print was taken from a book published by Alardt in Amsterdam.

There is in the British Museum what is recognized as the earliest map of New York and known as " The Duke's Plan." This is entitled " A Description of the Towne of Mannados or New Amsterdam as it was in September 1661 " ; for it will be recollected that after settlement had been commenced here by the Dutch West India Company in 1624, the name New Amsterdam was assigned to it until in 1664 it was seized by the English and, in honour of the Duke of York, its present name was given. The map is done in colours and gilt, very much in the style of the Batavia plan, with topography and shipping as seen from the air. Thus, the aviator who to-day makes photographic surveys, is merely following along an old tradition.

Finally we have two more Dutch prints which were done for the booksellers, and aid us in living again with the shipmen of the past. The first was engraved by the Amsterdam engraver Joseph Mulder, whose plates are dated over the period 1694 to 1737. He was one of those men who were called upon to do such diverse subjects as title-pages, portraits, views, as requirements insisted. The subject is the important base where the Dutch East Indiamen were built and fitted out. In the background is the big store, with the carpenters' yard in front. One East Indiaman is on the stocks being planked up, and a typical yacht, such as was used for navigating Dutch waters, is further to the right. She has no boom, the yard is " standing," there are twin-vangs on either side ; these with the leeboards and the windowed cabin aft are all shown with historical accuracy. On her flag are the letters " O.A.C." indicating the East Asiatic Company. The second print shows the same base with one of the company's ships which has been on fire. The men with their hoses and pumps are discernible in the foreground.

Thus the English, Dutch and French engravers of the seventeenth century found plenty of work now that printing had become so popular, and many people were attracted by the sea. All three countries were building up fine fleets, and the meaning of naval power was being well assimilated. It was a period of transition not merely in art and process methods, but in respect to ship-building and naval tactics, and the European settlement of nations. The Elizabethans understood more about handling ships than building them : they appreciated strategy more than fleet-tactics, they respected the boarding-pike more than the gun. But from the Anglo-Dutch wars there emerged better and more scientific naval architecture, the practice of employing ships in line-ahead so as to give the fullest play for their guns and allow a fleet to be used as a whole rather than as a series of independent units.   Signalling, discipline, administration, payment of officers and men, professional ability afloat—all needed much hard work and reform before efficiency could be obtained : but by the time the Dutch wars ended with the Peace of London in 1674 these items had begun to receive their necessary attention. As Pepys in his *Memoires of the Royal Navy* remarked, the " integrity and general (but unpractic'd) knowledge are not alone sufficient to conduct and support a Navy " ; yet through an age of incompetency and indifferent morality the English Navy comes past the test so triumphantly as to give the country a unique place among nations. But the influence of Jean Baptiste Colbert in his effort to produce for France a strong navy, with overseas colonization and extended commerce, was to be felt during the succeeding years, and thus create new rivalries, further sea wars, and an increased demand for those artists who could make naval battles intelligible to landsmen.

CHAPTER VI

MEZZOTINT AND AQUATINT

WHILST by his simple style and great technical skill such a real artist as Nooms was able to provide telling illustrations of contemporary ships, yet etching was employed by these Dutch exponents of seafaring only infrequently. The influence of the Low Countries on the English prints was not yet dead. Amsterdam and Antwerp sent some of their workers across to London, but not all were of the best grade. Michiel Van der Gucht, for example, who had been born at Antwerp in 1660, engraved for the London booksellers such subjects as portraits and naval incidents and died in Bloomsbury during the year 1725, was certainly capable of very inferior work. And yet he was the master of George Vertue (1684—1756), who achieved great fame as an English engraver.

There was born at Harlem in the same year as Van der Gucht an engraver and painter whose prints are highly esteemed to this day. This was Cornelis Dusart, who made both etchings and mezzotints, chiefly from peasant life but with a keen sense of caricature, as will be seen from the illustration "Man with a Rocket." Dusart's mezzotints can still be picked up for a pound or two, but this example is both rare and unusually interesting. It was done by him after one of his own designs, somewhere about 1690, and he ended his life in 1704. The well-known dangers of the Dutch coast with its numerous shoals and low-lying land required, on certain dark stormy nights, the use of these rockets for the safety of mariners.

The figure shown standing on a sea-wall, wearing in his hat a flag, has been supplied with half a dozen fireworks, one of which he is about to use ; but to some readers this incident may appear strangely modern. The fact is that pyrotechnics will be found far older than this print. Captain John Smith, in the early days of Virginia, did not hesitate to employ them as a means of impressing the Indians ; but the Dutch had a great love for letting off gunpowder on the occasions of their sham-fights and aquatic displays when yachts and other vessels paraded their waterways for show. The seventeenth-century warships, both English and Dutch, were notoriously wasteful of powder : it seemed to be an essential of hospitality that no distinguished guest should be received aboard except with the explosion of some charge. But eventually common sense insisted on economy.

There were among Dusart's contemporary countrymen, who were fellow-mezzotinters, such exponents as Gerard Valck (1626—1720), Jan van Somer (born in 1641), Jan Verkolje (1650—1693), and Abraham Blooteling (1640—1690), of whom the first, second, and fourth came over to England, where the new art became so firmly established that it was known as " la manière anglaise," its tonal quality making it particularly suitable as a method for reproducing paintings, but especially portraits. Thus, when we come to the eighteenth century, we find well-known admirals commemorated in this manner. As an instance, there is J. Walker's portrait of Sir Hyde Parker (published in 1780) after Romney, and there are many others of Rodney, Hood, Howe, St. Vincent, Nelson.

The first English painter of standing to produce in oil our naval achievements was one Isaac Sailmaker, who was born in 1633. None of his pictures has been preserved, but Van der Gucht and others made engravings and these fetch high prices to-day. Some

Dutch mezzotinters, as for example Abraham Blooteling just mentioned, were also eminent line-engravers. I have thought well to include in our reproductions the line-engraving published at Amsterdam about 1705 showing in part the sphere of operations in the War of the Spanish Succession. An alliance having been made between England, Holland and Austria, hostilities proceeded on land as well as sea, the conduct of affairs afloat being under the command of Sir George Rooke. It was he who, at Vigo in 1702, destroyed the French and Spanish fleets, in 1704 captured Gibraltar, and defeated the French in the Battle of Malaga, which is in a bay to the east of Gibraltar. When, after much fighting, this tiresome war was concluded in 1713 by the Peace of Utrecht, England was able to retain Gibraltar and Minorca in Europe ; Hudson's Bay, Nova Scotia, and Newfoundland across the Atlantic.

This print is a late example of that method of making a map lively and more interesting, by covering the sea with ships. By reason of the necessary reduction these have come out not very distinctly, but in the original they are seen to great advantage. The three-masters, the fore-and-aft rigged sloops, and the barges under single squaresail, have all been done with great delicacy. Pierre Mortier's dedicatory inscription on the right-hand corner says that the print has been " dressé sur les memoires des plus habiles ingenieurs." There is in existence a plan-like print of Rooke's capture of Vigo (1702) which is worth studying with the above. The title says that " . . . This Draught was taken by L. du Meé Ingenieur put out by the order of the States of Holland " ; and at the bottom left-hand corner that it is " Sold by David Mortier Book Seller at yᵉ Sign of Erasmus's head near the Fountain Tavern in the Strand." In P. Mortier's Spanish map the reader will note the words, " Avec Privilege." On many other prints " cum privilegio " will likewise be found. This alludes to the special right to publish, granted by a political or (in some cases) ecclesiastical authority. It was in effect a kind of copyright.

During the first quarter of the eighteenth century there flourished Thomas Baston, who deserves our attention because he has left us some very spirited illustrations of English men-of-war. Himself a seascape painter, he also did a few etchings from his own designs, but some of his pictures were engraved by Harris, Kirkall, and others. A desirable Baston series is that entitled *Twenty-two Prints of several of the Capital ships of his Majesties Royal Navy*, which will be found in the Print Room of the British Museum. The detail of these " wooden walls," with their great topsails and their picturesque poop lanterns, is most valuable if we wish to study the ships of the period immediately preceding 1765, the date when Nelson's *Victory* was launched. The print before us, showing seven English men-of-war beating to windward, was engraved by J. Sartor after Baston's draught, and it contains several points which will arrest the ship-lover's eye.

In the first place we notice—as we learn also from contemporary documents—that these unhandy craft could not sail close to the wind. That old-fashioned mizzen sail is the same lateen which such vessels as Columbus' *Santa Maria* had derived from the Mediterranean galleys. Handed on through the sixteenth and seventeenth centuries, it has indeed become quadrilateral rather than triangular, yet it is but slightly modified. Notice, too, the Jack flying forward. Although the union of Scotland and England had taken place in 1707, it was not until 1801 that the Union Jack was altered by the introduction of a saltire for the union of Ireland with Great Britain. By the middle of this eighteenth century staysails and triangular headsails were no longer exceptional, though the spritsail was retained below the highly-steeved bowsprit as

OSP—G

Baston has indicated. The sprit topmast flying the Jack had presently to disappear when going to sea, for it was in the way of the big jib that was about to be introduced ; but when in harbour, or at anchor, the jackstaff was retained, just as in His Majesty's ships to-day the Union Jack is at once hoisted on anchoring and lowered before getting under way. In Baston's reproduction the fore staysail is still a very small affair. Such details as the running and standing rigging, the pennants, the stowage of the anchors, and the t'gallant yards are features which immediately attract our attention, and the artist has shown the crashing effect of those clumsy bows butting into a head sea. Certainly such prints as this give a life and meaning to eighteenth-century naval history, for they help us to visualize the manner in which fleets went into action, or fought their way across the ocean under conditions that we can scarcely envy.

The relation between mezzotint and colour should now be emphasized. At its best the former is really a practicable convention which endeavours to reproduce in white and black the qualities of a painting ; but a convention is one of those tacit agreements by which a certain meaning is generally accepted, quite apart from the question of truth. By means of the imagination and educated taste we are able to endow a mezzotint with tone and colour : the most sensitively artistic mind perceives more than any other. But the desire to produce actual prints in colour was bound to come eventually. The first experiments in the employment of the three-colour process for mezzotint plates were made by another of those alien craftsmen, and his name was J. C. Le Blon. His life was spent in Paris, Amsterdam, Rome, Frankfort, as well as London, his period being 1667 to 1741. Possibly the first Englishman to experiment with colour printing was Elisha Kirkall, who was born at Sheffield in 1685 and died at Whitefriars, London, in 1742.

He worked in both mezzotint and chiaroscuro and did such hackneyed subjects as that incident when Hollar was nearly captured by the Algerine pirates, the Battle of Solebay, and the Four Days' Fight of 1666.

These early efforts were very crude, and we shall note that the French engravers were scarcely more successful. Let us take, for example, Pierre Fourdrinier, who came to England and for about thirty years remained in London engraving many plates till he died there in the year 1758. The Hollar affair had created a kind of melodramatic standard which required a long time to kill, for, of all things in the world, the late seventeenth century and the next hundred years were entirely lacking in originality. Thus, when P. Monemie's painting of " A Sea Engagement between the English and Algerines " had been exhibited in Vauxhall Gardens, the commission came to Fourdrinier to reproduce it. This line-engraving coloured was published in 1743 by Thomas Bowles, the well-known London engraver and printseller, but neither as a work of art nor as a faithful representation of ships can it possibly please. It is, however, possible to recommend such mezzotints as that sentimental " William's Farewell to Black-Eyed Susan." Artist, engraver, and publisher are the same three just mentioned, but the inspirer was John Gay, the poet who wrote *The Beggar's Opera* and such ballads as " Black-Eyed Susan," " 'Twas when the Seas were Roaring." For this was the period when they buried such people in Westminster Abbey ; when insincerity was the chief characteristic of manners and morals ; when deeds were more swayed by shallow emotions than by reason, with the inevitable disastrous reactions.

On the other hand the lot of the sailor was bearable simply because it gave a chance to travel and to fight. The " death-or-glory " spirit manifested itself in art, drama and literature ; the sailor became a national standardized hero; his name was synonymous with bravery afloat and wild behaviour ashore; his ships and naval occasions brought increasing work to painters and engravers. Thus such enterprising people as Thomas Bowles was able to issue engravings of Admiral Vernon's Capture of Porto Bello (1739) within five months of the incident, just as to-day the newspaper Press supplies us with illustrations of yesterday's events. The engraver-printseller W. H. Toms, who lived near Hatton Garden, Holborn, took advantage of the notorious engagement off Toulon (February 22, 1744) to give the public a detailed print showing a bird's-eye view of the English, French and Spanish fleets when the engagement began. The subsequent political storm in England concerning the behaviour of Admirals Lestock and Mathews on this occasion, the bickerings and innuendoes, the courts-martial and gross injustice which stirred up the public spirit, also created a desire to see what it was all about. It was thus that the engravers were becoming of greater importance in social life, for the parochial outlook was gradually being overcome.

One cannot too greatly emphasize the importance of maintaining an intimate relation between prints and history. The collection merely as a bundle of illustrations is meaningless; but when we regard them side by side with the great movements that were going on at the time, both the prints themselves and the events take on an irresistible human interest. Therefore these ship illustrations must be regarded as only parts of the big record. Art for art's sake sounds very well, but we shall miss the very source of the inspiring motive if we do not remember collaterally the feeling of international suspense during this eighteenth century, the parliamentary upheavals at home, the bloodshed on sea, the clashing of interests and rivalries between France and England in respect of the East and West Indies. These designs of naval actions, or single ships, were the results of intense feeling and of the few deep but sincere emotions which eighteenth-century people could exhibit. The hard, hollow rigid artificiality of social manners ashore was indeed universal, that it affected the mentality of great admirals afloat in the crisis of battle. Thus the letter of any regulation became more respected than the spirit, and Byng went into fight with the recollection that Mathews had been cashiered for daring to leave his line. The thought worried Byng, so that at the crucial moment when opposed to de la Galissonière the English admiral faltered, feared to risk a mistake, played for caution, and instead of pressing on to smash a retreating foe, hove-to and summoned a council of war. It was the hard formality of cast-iron tactics, the respect for convention, that had spoilt the day.

And yet, when we remember that artists painted all grass brown simply because it was the fashion so to do, why should we wonder? It needed many new movements in religion, in politics, in art, industry, naval tactics, naval architecture, and shipbuilding before the dead character of the eighteenth century could receive the true breath of life. The riots and uneasiness in England, the maladministration of public affairs, the notorious " rotten boroughs," the bribery and corruption of high officials, set going a demand for reform and economy which caused Burke to introduce his Bills that failed to receive Parliament's approval. It needed all Pitt's ability, his energy and good fortune to save the late eighteenth-century England from disaster; yet an agricultural country began to get a fresh lease of life through industrial machinery; coal and iron were to transform her ships and navy in the following decades. But mutinies in our own service, and the French Revolution abroad, sufficiently indicated that human nature was unable to endure the conditions which had long since become obsolete. In North America can we wonder that Congress had declared its States to

be independent of England ? Can any impartial historian to-day
deny that the whole cause of trouble between the English Government and the American colonists was identical with that which
was ruining art and the navy ; namely, a woeful lack of imagination ?

But it was Burke, also, who in one of his memorable speeches
referring to the colonies called attention to the neglected industry
of whaling. " And pray, sir, what in the world is equal to it ?
Pass by the other parts, and look at the manner in which the people of
New England have of late carried on the whale fishery ? " But
Englishmen, if still neglectful of South Sea whaling—that is to say
in the Pacific—had been for a long while pursuing the whale in the
neighbourhood of the Arctic, even as far back as the sixteenth
century. It was thus that such ports as London, Kingston-on-
Hull, Whitby, Newcastle, and Lynn came into especial prominence ;
but by the end of the eighteenth century Kingston-on-Hull was the
principal centre of this activity.

The line-engraving (Plate 26, above) showing the newly-
made basin for the latter's whaling ships belongs to this period, and
was done by B. F. Liezel in France. As a work of art it well shows
the conventionality and insincerity of which we have been speaking.
This is one of a pair that were published, and it is not to be despised,
for there has recently grown up a great demand for such a subject
as this. Whaling prints of any kind are comparatively few, but
fine quality items are exceedingly rare. Those who would aim
to make a comprehensive collection of whaling engravings may
begin with the sixteenth-century Dutch illustrations showing their
ships among the Arctic ice. During the eighteenth century quite
a number of indifferent line-engravings were published in England,
of which Plate 26, lower picture, engraved by R. Sheppard
is a fair example. It is entitled " The Greenland Whale Fishery,"
and in accordance with the sentimentalism of the age Sheppard

could not refrain from adding a wretched couplet : " Thus dies Leviathan, thus ends his Reign, O'er all th' inferiour Natives of the Main." But we must not forget that the whaling industry and everything connected therewith had a good deal of interest for some of our ancestors, who during the many vicissitudes of this fishery either lost or made fortunes. Hull was a famous whaling port right down till about the year 1868, and at the beginning of the nineteenth century was sending sixty ships to Greenland, the Davis Straits, and Spitzbergen. Similarly whalers to the South Seas used to sail out of London, the cost of fitting out such a type of vessel amounting to about £10,000, but she sometimes returned with 250 tuns of sperm oil valued at £24,000. An average cargo was about half that amount, but many shipowners living in the east and north-east ports of England and Scotland were interested in whaling expeditions, so that such printsellers as Carington Bowles of St. Paul's Churchyard published prints of these vessels frequently. There are plenty which show both English and Dutch vessels lancing, flensing, and hunting the whale. Harpooners in their oared boats, whales capsizing their pursuers among the bergs, and many another thrilling incident, were the kind of thing which the engravers illustrated.

The practical extinction of the sailing-ship whaler, coupled with the recently developed prosperity in the Antarctic through the use of steel steamships with guns, has thus given a new life to these old-time prints. No one can pretend that either Liezel or Sheppard's efforts convey anything but a crude idea of Greenland whalers, nor would one care to have such prints framed ; but they do help us to reconstruct past history and we must prize them in our collections as among the uncommon items. In America the last of the famous New Bedford whalers has disappeared into history, the fine race of whaler-skippers has passed away likewise ;

but later on in this volume will be mentioned an artist of French nationality who made pictures of this seafaring in the early years of the nineteenth century.

Some of the eighteenth-century coloured line-engravings have a decorative effect largely because they contain the stern of some ship with its ornate gilding, carvings, and windows. Such, for instance, is " The Capture of Louisbourg, June 1745," which was by J. Brooks after J. Stevens. The reason for such a plate was that the seizure of the town by New England troops from Boston, assisted by Sir Peter Warren's squadron, not merely destroyed a nest of French privateers and made matters easier for English fishermen working on the Banks, but caused a great moral impression. The view of New York as it appeared about the mid-eighteenth century, with an English ship in the foreground and the Jack flying over Fort George, is another coloured line-engraving which will always possess historical value, but is difficult to be found by the collector. This was published also by Bowles, the craftsman being J. Carwitham.

During this same century, when the French line-engravers were doing excellent work, there were not merely the book-illustrators such as H. F. Gravelot (1699—1773) and C. P. Marillier (1740—1808), but men like Charles Nicolas Cochin the younger, who was both engraver and painter as well. Belonging to the Watteau school, Cochin was very fond of using *fêtes galantes* for his subjects, but he was able also to try his hand at maritime subjects, of which "Port of Marseilles" (Plate 27) is a fine instance. It was engraved from one in a series of contemporary paintings belonging to the French king, which represented a collection of that country's ports. The artist was Claude Joseph Vernet, who was born at Avignon in 1714 and died in Paris during the year 1789. Himself the son of a painter-decorator, he specialized in themes concerning the sea. Associated with the younger Cochin in making this plate from Vernet's picture was Jacques Philippe Le Bas, who was accustomed to engrave portraits, historical and religious prints.

The subject-matter in this Marseilles print is intriguing. On one of those hot summer days when the wind is scant, a three-master is being towed out of harbour by her two boats with lines secured to the spritsail yard and inboard, at such a height that the ropes would clear the water. A light draught of air is filling the topsails, but the tartana trying to beat in has to use her oars. In the foreground of the picture, with its Watteauesque figures, the youths bathing, the man using a spy-glass, and the small craft rocking idly against the rocks, we have quite a fair idea of the delicate style which marked the late eighteenth-century manner. The date of the print is 1760.

It was Jean Baptiste Le Prince (1734—1784) who is reputed to have invented the process called aquatint, his earliest dated prints belonging to 1768. The earliest dated English aquatint belongs to 1771, being the work of P. P. Burdett of Liverpool, but the first to introduce the printing of aquatints in colour was François Janinet who lived in Paris from 1752 to 1813. Before the century ended aquatints had become very popular for reproducing colour pictures, and after 1790 we find them largely used in the illustrations of the colour books issued by the Boydells, Ackermann, Orme and other publishers. Just because this aquatint process rendered it possible to use plates suitable for colour printing there was at hand a means that would give people on shore a more realistic idea of the many-hued glints in naval battle-scenes, whose narrations were to occupy the public fears and hopes. It was all very well to hear the survivors' stories, but it meant far more when the marine artists and engravers of the time were able to present the

ships sailing in line-ahead ready to engage the enemy ; the red
and blue uniforms ; the ensigns and pennants bravely flying in
the sunlight ; the blue-green sea ; and the white puffs of smoke
belching from the guns.

Never were the old colour-prints so appreciated as they have
been ever since the twentieth century began, so that sensational
prices are asked and readily obtained. An early aquatint, here
reproduced plain (Plate 27), is called "The Thames at Limehouse."
Engraved by Johan Ziegler, it shows under way a three-masted
merchant ship with the old-fashioned square stern, and a not-too-
well-drawn Thames barge. Below the print is another couple of
doggerel verses which are typical of the period, for with the genuine
patriotic sea-fervour there is combined a sloppy effusive
sentimentalism which seems totally out of place with our present
standards of taste.

> O ! Thames, Thrice blest from hostile thunders free,
> Fed by the streams, and guarded by the sea,
> What charms can equal thine ? what bright array
> As white-wingd Traffic bears thy worth away ?
> While Gallant Navies on the bosom ride
> And brave their Redcross Pendants o'er thy Tide.
>
> While toils the Fisherman, with sturdy hand,
> Or hauls the net, or Aids his Native Land,
> May States, less blest, survey thy Tempted shore,
> Proclaim they beauties & thy matchless stores,
> As roll thy billows, to the distant brine,
> Still may thy Commerce own the hand divine.

Ziegler was born at Vienna in 1750, where he died in 1812. During
that period he brought out a number of etched and coloured views
of his native city : thirty-six colour-aquatints by himself and others
not long ago fetched about £60. The Thames print is one of a
pair and after Serres, its date being somewhere around 1780. Of
the latter family we shall see further work in another chapter

concerned with the fore-and-aft craft, but it will be convenient now to mention that here we have a late instance of marine art being carried on by father and sons.

For Dominique Serres, who was born at Auch in Gascony during the year 1722, ran away to sea, rose to become captain of a merchant vessel, and in the Thames illustration one can observe a sailor-like touch about the drawing of the three-master. Now, at the age of thirty, Serres and his ship were captured by the English, who brought him across the Channel. He devoted himself to art, acquired a reputation as a painter of sea-pieces as well as landscapes, and when the Royal Academy was instituted he was elected a member. Later on he was made marine painter to George III, and died in 1793.

But Serres left behind two sons, of whom Dominic was the younger, a water-colour draughtsman yet better known as a teacher of drawing. His life, like so many of these artists, ended in tragedy ; for his brain became overshadowed by despondency, he was no longer required as a teacher, and finally he had to be supported by his brother John Thomas Serres. The latter was born in London during the year 1759, and lived to become both marine painter to the King as well as draughtsman to the Admiralty. In 1801 he published *The Little Sea Torch for Coasting Ships*, with coloured plates, and four years later he brought out his *Liber Nauticus* as a handbook for painters. This is now an exceedingly rare work containing forty-one plates, but reproductions will be found in a later chapter. Unfortunately his last years were ruined by the depravity and extravagance of his wife, he became bankrupt, and died in 1825.

After Rodney and Hood had saved the West Indies and restored England to her position as mistress of the seas and the first nation of the world ; after peace eventually had come with the Treaty of Versailles in 1783, by which the possessions remained pretty much as before—save that England had to give back Minorca to Spain—there seemed some hope that both for the Navy and the English nation in general there might be a lasting peace. But in 1789 came the French Revolution, in January 1793 Louis XVI was executed, and in the following month Pitt was forced into war with France. Now, in order to appreciate the tension in England during the ensuing years, we must not forget that the French Navy had become by 1780 extremely efficient in regard to seamanship and signalling, as Kempenfelt pointed out by letter to the Admiralty ; but in 1790 the English Navy had once more learned from her rivals, adopted a new signal code and tactical system, on which all the great actions of the Nelson period were to be based. It is a significant fact that up to the year 1782 no important book on naval tactics had been published in English except for translations from the French.

But by the spring of 1794 the previously excellent French fleet was in that inferior condition which usually follows in the wake of a revolution. Discipline, seamanship, gunnery had all deteriorated, yet a violent appeal was made to urge the fighting temperament of the Frenchmen by inspiring hatred against England and by creating fear of being punished for failure to succeed. During the winter of 1793-1794 the English Channel Fleet had remained at anchor, but in readiness to put to sea as soon as our cruisers off the French coast should report that the enemy had come out of Brest. When the spring arrived, there was activity afloat which finally culminated in the battle that is always known as " The Glorious First of June," and began at about 9 a.m. Two and a half hours later twelve French ships out of twenty-five had been crippled ; and eleven English ships had been dismasted in Howe's fleet out of twenty-six ships-of-the-line, six frigates and six small craft. Soon after one o'clock general firing ceased, and later on Howe with part of his fleet and prizes sailed off to Spithead.

Such an incident as this not unnaturally inspired numerous artists and engravers, such as W. Elmes, N. Pocock, R. Pollard, H. W. Pearce, F. Weber, J. Theophilus, M. Brown, T. Luny and others : so that there exist in pairs, or sets of four, a good many engravings of a victory which aroused in England wild excitement. One may cite that rare stipple-engraving in colour which was done by Daniel Orme after Mather Brown. This is a very beautiful piece of work, in which the colouring is soft and glowing, the draughtsmanship first-class. The lighting and contrasts, the balance and grouping are all well done. On the other hand this is clearly the work of a portrait painter rather than of a genuine marine artist. The uniforms are spotless, as if no action had ever been fought, the faces bear little evidence of recent anxiety and suspense, the general pose is more dramatic than natural. But for all that no collector would willingly lose the chance of owning such a lovely print.

Mather Brown had been born in America in the mid-eighteenth century, and possibly at Boston. Having come to England when quite young, he was destined to be a pupil of his fellow-country-man Benjamin West (who succeeded Sir Joshua Reynolds as President of the Royal Academy). Brown painted portraits of George III, as well as many distinguished naval and military officers, such as Rodney and Cornwallis. His end is another tragedy, for he became almost an imbecile in his later days and died in London during the year 1831. Daniel Orme engraved in stipple many other portraits of celebrated contemporaries, but he also did miniatures and water-colour drawings. (There is one of the latter in the South Kensington Museum, dated 1799, showing Margate New Pier.)

Later mezzotinters of the third quarter of the nineteenth century sometimes combined line or stipple with mezzotint, but generally speaking the use of dots can be traced back to the sixteenth century goldsmith engravers. It is from the Italian Francesco Bartolozzi, who settled in London during 1764, that there was inaugurated a distinct school of English artists who adopted the stipple method, and no process was ever more suited for producing clear colour prints. One of a pair of aquatints of this same " Glorious First of June " published in 1795 is here reproduced, after the print by Robert Dodd, who was marine painter, engraver, and also publisher. During the latter part of the eighteenth century Dodd was a highly successful artist who enabled the nation to see how well its fleet had behaved in the great naval battles of the 'eighties, 'nineties, and early nineteenth century. Thus we can still go afloat with Parker, Rodney, St. Vincent, Nelson, and their gallant crowd ; for Dodd really knew how to paint ships in action. They are not dull, stupid, conventional things such as we have considered early in this chapter, but full of life and individualized character. The waves are not usually well done, for he was more concerned with accuracy of sails and rigging, getting the multi-gunned wooden walls into their battle positions, or presenting the tactical crises of the engagements. This, of course, was exactly what officers and their relatives required for proudly hanging up in their dining-rooms. It was a selected moment, such as the first impact with the enemy, which mattered, and the time had not yet come when the sincere independent interpretation of the sea's majesty and personality had been attempted, although Dodd certainly did depict such subjects as storms.

It is because of his ship-technique that Dodd's engravings have continued to increase their value during the present boom in nautical antiquities, but we can only appreciate adequately their contemporary relation to national excitement by recalling that same kind of anxiety which was felt in England during the late summer and autumn of 1914 when the Channel ports were being threatened by the German armies and the invasion of England was being made a likely possibility. In the year 1797 France attempted an invasion of Ireland; the fleets of France, Spain and Holland were to join hands off Brest and drive our fleet out of the Channel. After that fulfilment it was easy enough to see what would quickly follow. The expedition to Bantry Bay, however, failed and returned to Brest, but there were about a dozen line-of-battle ships in Toulon, twenty-seven Spanish sail in Cartagena, and about another dozen in Cadiz fitting out. Jervis and Nelson were separated with the enemy's fleet in between, for Nelson had been sent with a squadron of frigates to bring away from Elba the dockyard establishment, and was expected to pass through the Gibraltar Straits any day. Jervis therefore took up a cruising position from five to fifteen leagues south of Cape St. Vincent. Here on February 10 Jervis knew not merely that the Cartagena fleet had come through the Straits with a strong easterly wind, but that they had been driven to leeward of Cadiz. On the morning of February 13, Nelson, having sailed through the enemy, joined Jervis off the historic headland of St. Vincent on which Drake and his officers had so often gazed.

During the morning of the 14th the wind came westerly, the English and Spanish fleets sighted each other; at 10 a.m. de Cordova, the Spanish Commander-in-Chief, cleared for action, and the famous Battle of St. Vincent followed, a little before noon, as the fog (which had been hanging about) cleared away. The details of this occasion and of Nelson's brilliant bravery at a critical moment are well known, and about 5 p.m. the action had ended in an English victory. The effect on the Government and people of England was one of relief and outstanding joy. The former showered honours on the conquering fleet, so that Jervis became the Earl of St. Vincent. Nelson could have had a baronetcy but preferred the Ribbon of the Bath.

Now, with all this immense emotional enthusiasm in England there came plenty of work for such artists as Dodd to set down some of the aspects of the battle whilst yet the events were fresh to the mind. He wasted no time and by June 21 of that same year had published a pair of aquatints in colour, one of which showed the moment between four and five p.m. when Jervis' flagship *Victory* was ranging up astern of the 112-gun *Salvador del Mundo*. Both the painting and engraving had been done by the same artist, and if the surface of the sea is again unreal, suggestive rather of ruffled drapery than the deep Atlantic swell, there is something about the shell-shot sails and ensigns, the picturesque hulls and stern-galleries, that appeal to our imagination.

In the next year people at home were still kept constantly reminded that it was possible for catastrophe to happen should the Navy fail. Never for a month could the nation fail to realize that the sea and ships were her basic interest. What with the duties of dominating the Dutch fleet off the Texel, the Spanish fleet in Cadiz, the French fleet in Brest ; being ready to send other ships to thwart a landing in Ireland ; and, further, to protect merchant vessels from French privateers, there had been quite enough to prevent any languishing attention. And then there came that invasion bogey again, as it had two centuries previously, but this time the personified enemy was Napoleon. At various places between Havre and the Texel a large army was to be embarked, and sent across under cover of darkness and thick weather. But this could be rendered possible only if England's fleet should lose command of the sea.

(Page 88)

WHALING SHIPS AT KINGSTON-ON-HULL. *French line engraving in colour by* B. F. LIEZEL. *Eighteenth century.*

The Greenland Whale Fishery.
Thus dies Leviathan thus ends his Reign. *O'er all th' inferiour Natives of the Main.*

R. Sheppard Sculp.

(Page 88)

GREENLAND WHALERS. *Eighteenth century line engraving by* R. SHEPPARD.

PLATE 26

(Page 90) PORT OF MARSEILLES. *Line engraving by* C. N. COCHIN, 1760.

(Page 92) THE THAMES AT LIMEHOUSE. *Aquatint ın colour by* JOHAN ZIEGLER, *about* 1780, *after* D. SERRES.

PLATE 27

(Page 96)

BREAKING THE FRENCH LINE, JUNE 1, 1794. *Aquatint
after* ROBERT DODD'S *picture, published* 1795.

PLATE 28

(Page 106)

ACTION BETWEEN H.M.S. "PENELOPE" AND "GUILLAUME TELL,"
1800. *Aquatint in colour etched by* N. POCOCK, *and engraved by*
J. G. WELLS *after* POCOCK'S *design. Published* 1805.

PLATE 29

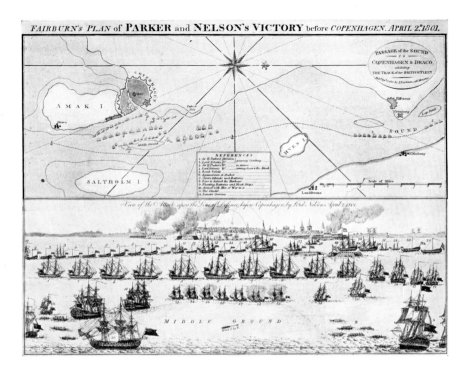

PLAN OF THE COPENHAGEN VICTORY, 1801.
From a coloured line engraving of the same year.

PLATE 30

(Page 117)

BATTLE OF COPENHAGEN, 1801. BRITISH FLEET APPROACHING.
Aquatint in colour, engraved by J. G. WELLS *and* R. POLLARD *after the picture by* N. POCOCK, 1801.

PLATE 31

(Page 122) ACTION IN THE BAY OF NAPLES, 1810. *From an aquatint in colour by* J. BAILEY *after* T. WHITCOMBE, *and published in* 1812.

(Page 123) ACTION BETWEEN H.M.S. "AMELIA" AND "L'ARETHUSE," 1813. *An aquatint in colour by* T. SUTHERLAND *after* T. WHIT-COMBE *and published in* 1817.

PLATE 32

(Page 127) BRITISH FRIGATE WITH CAPTAIN SIR HENRY HEATHCOTE'S STAYSAILS. *One of the early lithographs. Drawn on stone by* A. AGLIO *after* A. WEBB.

(Page 127) ACTION BETWEEN "NEPTUNO" AND "CAROLINA," 1826. *Aquatint in colour by* E. DUNCAN *after* W. JOY, *published* 1836.

PLATE 33

For a time this suspense kept the country of Nelson in a continuous state of alarm. Sailors and officers of the Royal Navy were regarded with an affection born of panic; the picture of a British man-of-war was a source of confidence. And then at the beginning of 1798 Napoleon, having rejected the invasion of England, aimed at conquering Egypt with a view to making a vast Eastern Empire that should include India and Turkey. During generation after generation the Honourable East India Company had built up the English Mercantile Marine and made England rich; but now came the threat to cut right across this important vein. Thus, again, was there every reason for nervousness at home. It was the Battle of the Nile which came as the inevitable collision of wills. It was this victory which saved British wealth, prestige, trade, shipping, and (to quote the words of that great admiral, Lord Hood) " preserved from anarchy, distress, and misery, the greatest part of Europe."

Therefore, once more came the sigh of relief, the shouts of joy, a still greater reliance on the Royal Navy, with a corresponding request for paintings, aquatints and line-engravings that might tell in English homes the story of this historic occasion. It was all for the good of marine art, and the printsellers were not slow to profit by the opportunity. Dodd was one of those who set to work and produced by the next year four aquatints in colour to illustrate important phases of the Nile battle. The surface of the sea is still conventional, but the arrangement of the ships is life-like. This series of plates is still so highly esteemed that they fetch sixteen, twenty-five and even a hundred guineas to-day.

The victory of Trafalgar, the great " annihilation " that the country (to quote Pitt) demanded over the enemy; the loss of the greatest sailor whom England ever owned; the secure primacy which Great Britain had now won among nations, and the long-desired peace that after generations of wars had finally come to our forefathers by means of the sea, gave an additional impulse to marine art which lasted right through till the clipper period and the advent of steam. Thus, long after the event, pictures were produced by men who had to do their best with such genuine data as they could obtain. Of Trafalgar artists there are plenty, but presently we are to consider the affair between the British 44-gun frigate *Indefatigable*, the British 36-gun frigate *Amazon*, and the French 74 *Droits-de-l'Homme*, which occurred in January 1797.

From the series of events which will be mentioned, here was just a subject as would delight the British public and inspire the picture-makers. Such comparatively minor events as the naval operations during the Burmese War of 1824–1826 (when steam war vessels were for the first time employed); then in 1827 the destruction of the Turkish and Egyptian fleets by the British, French and Russian at the Battle of Navarino to secure the independence of Greece; and the campaign of 1829 off the West African coast to suppress the notorious slave-trade, continued the effect of sustaining naval enthusiasm among those who were now profiting by the industrial prosperity.

No happier combination of painter and engraver emerged from this period than that of William John Huggins and Edward Duncan. The former came into the world during the year 1781. At an early age he went to sea in one of the Honourable East India Company's ships and was thus able to study at first hand the behaviour and handling of vessels under all weathers. Of his paintings we get a fair idea from three which he did in 1830 and following year of H.M. Brig *Black Joke*, H.M. Schooner *Pickle* and H.M. Brig *Primrose*, when at different dates in 1829 and 1830, a slave brig, schooner and frigate were taken captive. Huggins also made three pictures of Trafalgar, which are to be seen in

Hampton Court. In 1834 he was of such eminence as to be appointed marine painter to William IV, and eleven years later he died.

Duncan was born in London during 1803 and was articled to Robert Havell the engraver, whom we shall mention again a little later. It was from Havell that Duncan learned how to do aquatints, but the pupil brought to the task something more than the ordinary ability of a craftsman. Edward Duncan was a watercolour painter of many subjects, yet of coast scenery and shipping especially. In addition to this he was an etcher, lithographer, and one of the finest aquatint engravers at a time when this art was at its very height. Unquestionably the best of his aquatints were those which reproduced Huggins's paintings, and we shall not always find elsewhere that same admirable characterization or atmosphere which he exhibited when collaborating with this painter.

The story of the *Indefatigable* and *Droits-de-l'Homme* is as follows. After the failure of the Bantry Bay expedition in January 1797, Commodore la Crosse made for the French coast in the last-mentioned vessel, intending to make his landfall at Belle Isle ; and on Friday, the 13th, believed himself to be about twenty-five leagues west of France, but the weather came on thick, so he altered course to the southward under easy sail, with the wind fresh on the starboard beam. At 1 p.m. to windward there loomed up through the fog a couple of vessels, which he took to be enemies. They were indeed the *Indefatigable* (Captain Sir Edward Pellew) and *Amazon* (Captain R. C. Reynolds). The wind and sea were rising rapidly, but the Frenchman carried on and tried to get away.

By 3.30 p.m. the two British ships had worked round to leeward on the enemy's bow so as to cut la Crosse off from the land. Three-quarters of an hour later the Frenchman (a two-decker without a poop) whilst sailing under increased sail and heeling over so that she was compelled to keep her lower-deck ports shut, suddenly was caught in a squall which carried away her maintopsail braces, fore and main topmasts. But within twenty minutes her people had cleared the guns of all wreckage, and under her courses and mizzen-topsail she was still doing five knots. At 5.30 p.m. the *Indefatigable* reached her, shortened sail to close-reefed topsails, hauled up close to the wind, exchanged a broadside, tried to pass ahead so as to rake the *Droits-de-l'Homme*, but the latter thwarted this manœuvre and delivered a broadside into the *Indefatigable's* stern. Owing to the heavy sea now running, the Frenchman had to keep shutting the lower ports almost as soon as opened, but even then she took in quite an appreciable amount. After another forty-five minutes of firing, the *Amazon* came ramping along under a press of sail and delivered a broadside from close range. At 7.30 p.m. both Englishmen got ahead and there was a lull of an hour whilst *Indefatigable* and the enemy made some repairs. In the meanwhile the wind had backed more to the southward.

Until 10.30 p.m. the two English ships, disposed on each of the enemy's bows, continued the action with the bigger vessel, when the two-decker carried away her mizzenmast. With slight intervals the engagement went on through the night under circumstances that necessitated excellent seamanship; and then at 4.20 a.m. the land close aboard suddenly, by a clearing of the moon, revealed itself. *Indefatigable* and *Amazon* managed to haul off after a long and fatiguing engagement, during which the crew on the main deck of each frigate had been working with the sea up to their middles. *Indefatigable* had four feet of water in her hold, the *Amazon* had three feet, but both were badly damaged as to their spars and had lost a number of men. The land could not then be identified, but we know that it was at Audierne Bay, some distance to the southward of Brest. When daylight came at 6.30 a.m. it was seen that the *Droits-de-l'Homme* had failed to claw off—she had got into shoal water, and there she lay on her beam ends with a terrible surf frothing over her.

Indefatigable managed to get clear of dangers and out to sea, but *Amazon* presently had been driven to leeward, hit the ground and became a total loss, most of her crew escaping to the shore in rafts, where they were promptly made prisoners and marched into Audierne.   As to *Droits-de-l'Homme*, she had fetched up on a sand-bank, and it was not till the fourth day that so many as survived death were rescued by the arrival of a man-of-war and cutter who anchored and sent their boats to the wreck.   Finally, by this means and large rafts, the rescue efforts were rewarded, though many lives had been lost.

Such is the thrilling story which Huggins painted and Duncan engraved, and they selected the evening of that memorable Friday, the thirteenth of January, at the time when the *Amazon* (in the right background) was hurrying up, but *Indefatigable* was already engaging the *Droits-de-l'Homme*.   This print may be compared with that other here reproduced, entitled " South Sea Whale Fishery," which also is in colour and was engraved in 1836 by Duncan after the picture by Ambroise Louis Garneray.   The aquatint before us is one of a pair that are very rarely found, especially in colour, though copies of a smaller size do exist.   Garneray was a distinguished French marine painter who passed through many adventures afloat.   Born in Paris during the year 1783, he went to sea when only thirteen, and ten years later was taken prisoner by the English.   After remaining in England until 1814, he returned to France where he enjoyed the patronage of Louis XVIII.   He studied the art of aquatint, designed and engraved sixty-four views of the principal French ports, which were published in 1821–1832.   In the following year he was made Director of Rouen Museum, where there hangs his picture which he painted in 1839, entitled " Cod Fishing off Newfoundland." A number of books also appeared with his name, such as his *Voyages, adventures et combats* (Paris, 1851), *Voyages de Garneray* (Paris, 1853), *Scenes Maritimes* (Paris, 1863).

The incident that concerns us is such as was by no means infrequent during the days of the sailing-ship whalers. After the look-out man from his perch aloft at the whaler's masthead had suddenly startled every one with the cry, " There she blows ! " and answered the captain's bellowing, " Where away ? " by the reply, " Two points on the lee bow, sir," there would be a hurry and scurrying on deck. The main topsail would be backed, the boats lowered away, and under sail or oars they went racing off to the school of cachalots. A cool steersman and a harpooner who knew his job were essential at the moment of contact with the whale. But if the least mistake occurred through nervousness, lack of experience, or accident, then as likely as not the boat and men would receive disaster. There were two maxims among the whaling community which had to be learnt by new-comers : " A dead whale or a stove boat " reminded them that not both could inhabit the same locality for long. " Beware of a sperm's jaw, and a right whale's flukes." In Garneray's picture those terrible jaws have snapped in two the spritsail rigged boat, and its crew are leaping for the sea. In the distance to the left is the whaling ship, and another boat is running from her before the wind, so the men will have some chance of being picked up. In 1836 there was an almost similar incident when an American whaler in the South Seas had one of her boats nipped right in two, but by good fortune not one of the crew was injured. It may surprise some people that Garneray has depicted a boat going into action with sail still set ; but there were plenty of instances where the hurry was so great to reach the whale that this did happen, and it was not lowered until the harpoon had got deep down into the whale. But these men worked with minute fractions of safety, so that a puff of wind, a playful wave, an unexpected movement of the whale, or the steersman becoming " gallied " (*i.e.* alarmed through loss of nerve), would often cause a sharp, quick ending.

It is fortunate that so many painters and engravers during the period of the French wars were encouraged to record the great fleet actions, single-ship combats, the captures by privateers, the sailing of merchant convoys and so on. At a time when there was no illustrated press, and no electric telegraph, the eager public had to wait a long time for its information ; but this interval did afford to the artists an opportunity to get at the facts, to consult officers who had taken part in the operations. Such important events as the Battle of the Saints, the Battle in Quiberon Bay, Howe's victory off Ushant, the Battle of Camperdown, the attacks on Gibraltar, were all carefully reproduced. And a collector of prints about to start his hobby within restricted limits might do worse than confine himself to these French wars out of which British sea-power emerged triumphant. The old-time sailor always had a leaning towards art even if his technique was uninstructed ; but there were many who after coming ashore were taught to use their natural talents in such a manner that they could never paint a ship except with studied accuracy. Marine pictures will always belong to one of the most highly technical categories ; nothing is more ludicrous than a mere landsman fumbling about among what are meant to be rigging and practicable sails. But a hundred years ago the dividing line between the sailor and the rest of humanity was much more contrasted ; and no one was more critical than officer or man who had served in the ships depicted. There are, indeed, flagrant cases still existing in some of our galleries where ships are shown by first-class artists in positions that are historically wrong. Occasionally the vanity of the person who commissioned the painter, or the latter's false striving after effect, or his preference for grouping than for plain truth, was responsible for misrepresentation ; but in others it was owing to neglect of research after facts.

When a retired shipmaster takes to portraying marine subjects we can be pretty sure that his work is about as reliable as any human effort can make it. Thus when we come to Nicholas Pocock we can never be disappointed. Born during 1741 in that west-country port of Bristol, which had done so much for Atlantic shipping through the two previous centuries and was so intimately connected with the West Indian colonization, Pocock received command of a merchant ship and used to fill in part of his time on passage making sketches of what he beheld. After coming ashore altogether he devoted himself to art entirely, and was fortunate to win the notice of the great Sir Joshua Reynolds. At forty-one Pocock was already exhibiting his pictures at the Royal Academy ; seven years later he came up to London and was kept busy depicting those naval battles which made the next few decades so fateful to his country.

Pocock died in 1821, but such engravers as Francis Chesham and J. G. Wells have left to us prints of his work which are highly esteemed by collectors. It was Chesham who made the plate for Pocock's well-known " Battle of the Saints." That, however, which I have included for our contemplation is the delightful aquatint (see Plate 29), drawn and etched by Pocock, engraved by Wells, and published by Pocock in 1805. It is nowadays worth about fifteen guineas. Working in London from about 1785 to 1809, when he left to live in Norway, Wells was an active engraver by the aquatint method. Many of his plates are after his own

(Page 100)

H.M.S. "INDEFATIGABLE" ENGAGING THE FRENCH
"DROITS-DE-L'HOMME" 1797. *Aquatint in colour by*
E. DUNCAN *after* W. J. HUGGINS. *Published* 1829.

PLATE 34

(Page 103)

SOUTH SEA WHALE FISHERY. *Aquatint in colour*
by E. DUNCAN *after* A. L. GARNERAY. 1836.

PLATE 35

designs, but he did such naval subjects from other artists' works as the pair after Powell showing the " Action between H.M.S. *Pallas* and *La Minerve*." The " Battle of Copenhagen," in aquatint by Wells and Chesham, after the painting by Whitcombe, fetches from £3 to three times that amount. But the " Action between H.M.S. *Penelope* and *Guillaume Tell*," after Powell, is a print which changes hands for as much as £75. This same incident is used for the Wells-Pocock aquatint in colour, here reproduced plain. The reason why this subject was so popular will be immediately understood.

In 1798 Malta had been taken by the French before the Battle of the Nile (which occurred in August). After the Nile victory there followed the British blockade of Alexandria ; but, owing to the bad autumn weather and the coastal dangers which caused the loss of the small blockading vessels, this operation had to be relinquished. From the middle of October an effective blockade of Malta had, however, commenced, and in the harbour of Valetta there lay with other ships the 80-gun *Guillaume Tell*, flagship of the French Admiral Decrès. We may pass over the ensuing months until the spring of 1800, by which time supplies on the island had become very low, and it was determined that Admiral Decrès in the *Guillaume Tell* should endeavour to break through to France with news that Malta could not hold out longer than June.

On March 30 the British naval force off the island consisted of the 80-gun *Foudroyant*, the 74-gun *Alexander*, the 64-gun *Lion* and the 36-gun frigate *Penelope*, as well as a handful of small craft. The night was dark, the moon had set, a strong southerly gale was blowing, and Decrès put to sea on his plucky but difficult mission. Let us realize that we are to witness a night action in which on both sides there was a magnificent display of resource, perseverance, gallantry, and real seamanship. It was 11 p.m. when the French-man weighed from Valetta, whilst outside there lay at anchor the *Lion*; to leeward were *Foudroyant* and *Alexander*, but *Penelope* (Captain Henry Blackwood *) was patrolling between *Lion* and the harbour mouth.

A few minutes before midnight *Penelope* sighted *Guillaume Tell* to windward coming along under a great press of sail. Captain Blackwood immediately sent the brig *Minorca* to inform the senior officer of the blockading squadron, and as soon as the enemy had passed, tacked and stood after her. After about half an hour *Penelope* had reached *Guillaume Tell* and poured in a broadside, but Decrès continued to hurry on to the north and east. *Penelope*, being the faster and being beautifully handled, was able to keep up a raking fire with her broadsides so that just before dawn the French ship lost her main and mizzen topmasts as well as main yard. This condition will be observed in the reproduction, and by clever seamanship Captain Blackwood had avoided exposing his vessel to the enemy's superior fire. In the meanwhile *Lion* had slipped her cable and got under way after dispatching *Minorca* to inform her two sisters, and whilst tearing along through the boisterous darkness kept sending up rockets and blue lights as a help to those ships coming up astern.

About 5 a.m. *Lion* came up between *Penelope* and *Guillaume Tell*, gave the latter a broadside thrice and then luffed across the enemy's bows, carrying away the crippled Frenchman's jib-boom and raking him fore-and-aft. But presently *Lion* received such heavy damage that she dropped astern out of control. At 6 a.m.

---

* An extremely efficient officer who had considerable experience in frigates. It was he who, five years later, was sent by Collingwood to England with news of the French fleet. On his way to the Admiralty, after landing, he called at Merton, where the well-known meeting took place with Nelson, who a fortnight later set out from Portsmouth for his last campaign.

arrived *Foudroyant*, who had slipped from her anchorage about midnight, and she came romping on with so much sail that she shot ahead of *Guillaume Tell*, who refused to strike her colours when asked, and both ships exchanged broadsides. *Foudroyant* in this phase lost her foretopmast, maintopsail yard, jib-boom and sprit-sail yard, with foresail, mainsail and staysail all in tatters. She dropped astern, but *Lion* and *Penelope* were still keeping up the combat. At 6.30 a.m. the *Guillaume Tell* was still further disabled by the loss of her main and mizzen masts, and then *Foudroyant*, after temporary repairs, again attacked. In less than two hours Decrès' ship had lost her foremast and was nothing but a helpless wreck rolling violently, as a ship always does after being entirely dismasted. Finally, unable to use her guns, she hauled down her colours.

Foudroyant and *Lion* being too maimed, it was *Penelope* who took the prize in tow and brought her to Syracuse. Later on *Guillaume Tell* was sent to Portsmouth and it is easy enough to realize why in Trafalgar year Pocock published a print concerning so gallant an episode. " A more heroic defence than that of the *Guillaume Tell*," wrote the great naval historian James, " is not to be found among the records of naval actions. . . . Without Captain Blackwood's promptitude, gallantry, and perseverance . . . the *Guillaume Tell* would most probably have escaped." The latter was the only line-of-battle ship which had remained to the French after the Battle of the Nile, and her loss, therefore, still further depressed the spirits of the Valetta garrison. Thus, when the dogs and cats had been consumed as food, Malta was compelled in the following September to capitulate to the British, in whose hands she has continued to remain.

These old ship prints, therefore, are bound up with the great moments of sea history ; and what the mezzotints did for the honourable remembrance of admirals, the aquatints especially effected for the sea-fights which thrill us to-day as they roused the admiration of our forefathers. We can now proceed to consider how during the early nineteenth century naval actions and life in merchantmen were reported by engravers just before the steamship was to rob the sea of that romantic sail-clouded vessel which has controlled the world's development in respect of discovery, conquest, trade, and colonization.

CHAPTER VII

EARLY NINETEENTH-CENTURY SHIP PRINTS

WHILST we look to the Dutch engravers for our principal source of illustrative knowledge concerning ships of the sixteenth and seventeenth centuries ; whilst, too, the transition period (when English craftsmen and artists were applying the lessons learned from foreigners) is not bereft of invaluable sea prints ; yet it was only with the introduction of aquatints that we were able to reach a technical excellence worthy of stirring maritime achievements.

At the beginning of the nineteenth century there was not too much encouragement for the æsthetic side of life, since the whole of Europe seemed occupied with warfare. From the north of that continent to the Mediterranean, from Asia to the Atlantic, men were drawn from the pursuits of peace to destroy and not to create. Life is not a poetic idyll but a powerful drama, and the story of the world is largely that of struggle against obstacles human or natural. But four millions of men were now being employed in military service, and national energies were being drained at the expense of infant industries.

Still events incite curiosity for greater information, and the growing popularity of the press had been marked by the appearance of *The Times* newspaper in 1788. The official *London Gazette* had indeed been started as far back as 1665, and in this organ the anxious early nineteenth-century public could find the naval dispatches sent from the seat of war; but for minds unable to read they were not the same illuminating influence which a picture or engraving provided. Unofficial newspapers were barely able to keep going under official prosecution, such as that for having printed an article against flogging in the Army. Moreover, the heavy stamp duty made it necessary to charge sevenpence for a daily paper. This made news dear enough for the wealthy, but prohibitive for others when (as happened in 1801) the cost of a quartern loaf rose to one shilling and tenpence, and there was no imported grain to relieve the situation.

In these circumstances he who could issue at a moderate price some sort of illustrated sheet to supplement admirals' statements was doing a popular act; for what with poverty and taxation, our difficulties in trading abroad, and the Napoleonic menace, the British nation heartily desired peace, but a settlement that could come only through victory after fighting. Therefore, whatever concerned the fleet interested the people, and the coloured line-engraving (here reproduced plain) indicates how quickly an enterprising printseller could respond to the prevailing demand.

This is Fairburn's plan of the Copenhagen victory, and seeing that the battle occurred only on April 2, 1801, yet this print was published by John Fairburn of the Minories, London, on April 22, one can perceive the haste which the circumstances insisted should be made. It was on April 15 that Parker's and Nelson's dispatches reached the Admiralty, and the same day they were issued in a *London Gazette* " Extraordinary." Thus Fairburn had only a week in which to get this plan drawn, coloured, and printed. Below it were the list of ships on both sides; the two admirals' dispatches, the list of British killed and wounded, together with the publisher's editorial that " This most brilliant and unexampled Victory was achieved by that invincible Son of Neptune and

Collosus of the Ocean, Lord Nelson, and the brave Officers and Men under his Command. . . ."

Those citizens who were illiterate could now have the facts read to them, could study the plan and the view, so that in short this broadsheet served the purpose of the modern newspaper which illustrates by its half-tone blocks. We must in fairness to Fairburn thus respect his endeavour to please anxious families of gallant sailors before we criticize his accuracy. Until this naval victory England had excited the illwill of the neutral states, Denmark, Russia, Sweden, and Prussia, and it was greatly feared that their combination would presently cease to be an armed neutrality but merge into an alliance with France. The political result of the Copenhagen campaign did, however, cause that dangerous neutrality's dissolution, and in 1802 France, being weary of war, signed with Britain the Peace of Amiens, though in effect it was to mean little more than an armistice.

It was by his old chief Lord St. Vincent, now First Lord of the Admiralty, that Nelson had been sent as second-in-command under Sir Hyde Parker to the Baltic ; but when the " Collosus of the Ocean " joined his fleet at Yarmouth he soon saw that Parker was " a little nervous about dark nights and fields of ice." Nor was Nelson quite happy in the restrictions imposed by hydrographical conditions. " I experienced in the Sound," wrote the latter, " the misery of having the honour of our country entrusted to a set of pilots who have no other thought than to keep the ships clear of danger, and their own silly heads clear of shot." For the time had not yet come when the world should be furnished with the excellent charts of to-day. And it will be convenient here to sum up parenthetically the progress which had been made in regard to hydrography, since it has ever been so closely allied with the art of engraving.

As the reader is aware, Lucas Jansz Wagenaer of Enkhuisen had in 1583 published at Leyden his *Der Spieghel der Zeevaerdt*, of which an English edition was introduced three years later by Sir Anthony Ashley. Various other Dutchmen issued charts, but the first chartseller to set up in England as a nautical publisher was John Seller, during the reign of Charles II. His address was, The Sign of the Mariner's Compass, Hermitage Stairs, Wapping, where in 1670 he printed the first part of *The English Pilot ;* but, be it remembered, the copper plates of the charts in this series he had purchased from Holland. Seller then removed the Dutch titles and inscribed his own name instead. The title-page is original, though the inspiration owes something to Wagenaer's page. Thus the English title is set amid the figures of the great English adventurers Davis, Drake, Cavendish and Captain John Smith ; surrounded by globes, charts, compasses, dividers, the cross staff and quadrant as navigational adjuncts. There is a quite charming strip, showing the Thames at London Bridge with St. Paul's and the Tower, that is strangely similar to Hollar's work ; and at the foot of the page are engraved two ancient figures to denote Father Thames and Father Medway.

This *English Pilot* described " The Sea-Coasts, Capes, Headlands, Soundings, Sands, Shoals, Rocks and Dangers ; The Bayes, Roads, Harbours, Rivers and Ports in the Northern and Southern Navigation," and obtained for Seller the appointment of Hydrographer to the King. But also it won imitation at the hands of envious and dishonest persons. Now the manner among mariners had quite early caused those Dutch, Wagenaer-like charts to be known in England colloquially as " waggoners." Other sailormen spoke of them as " lightning columns " or " sea-torches," which was a fair description. In the twenty-third year of the reign of Charles II letters-patent were granted by His Majesty ensuring

Seller thirty years' copyright, and the following extracts show the privilege which engravers and printsellers sometimes enjoyed.

" Charles the Second, By the Grace of God, King of England. . . . Whereas We have been given to understand, that Our Trusty and Wellbeloved Subject, John Seller, Our Hydrographer in Ordinary, hath been for these several years last past, Collecting and composing two large Treatises of Navigation, the one Entitled the English Pilot, the other the Sea Atlas . . . a Work of very great Expence and Cost, and not heretofore performed in this Our Kingdom. The first Part whereof being now fully and entirely finished, We are informed that Endeavours are made by some of Our Subjects, secretly to Copy and Reprint the same, but under another Title, to the great prejudice and discouragement of the said John Seller. . . . We do by these presents strictly prohibit and forbid all Our Subjects. . . to Copy, Epitomize, or Reprint the said Treatises. . . . Or to Copy or Counterfeit any of the Maps, Plats, or Charts that shall be in the said Treatises, within the term of thirty years. . . . And that no such Books, Maps, Charts or Plats, or any Part or Copy thereof, be imported from beyond the Seas, either under the Name of Dutch Waggoners, or Lightning Columes, or under any other Name Whatsoever."

Seller's closely-protected business prospered, and with the expansion of the Mercantile Marine there grew up during the eighteenth century other British chart-producing firms, some of whose descendants are still engaged in London as publishers. The third part of Seller's *English Pilot* was issued in 1703, and the fourth came later. Thus private enterprise continued to provide mariners with their charts, though merchant ship masters and naval captains often enough made their own surveys, or added to the incomplete material already printed. After John Seller there followed in London a line of chart publishers through the ensuing generations. Thus John Senex, famous cosmographer, brought out before the mid-eighteenth century excellent nautical and scientific publications,

which caused him to be elected in 1728 a member of the Royal
Society. There was Phil Overton, there was Robert Sayer, and
then came Robert Laurie and James Whittle in the early nineteenth
century, who all produced revised editions or entirely new charts
and pilots. Through Sayer were issued the *North American Pilot*,
surveyed and drawn by that great navigator and discoverer Captain
Cook, in 1760–1766, and some of these actual copper-plates still
exist.

But it was largely owing to Sayer that hydrography became so
much improved during that eighteenth century. Such distinguished
men as Captain J. Huddart, F.R.S., who was born in 1741, served
in the Honourable East India Company's service for ten years, and
died in 1816, owed much of his fame as hydrographer to the
publicity which his works obtained through Sayer. In 1785,
for instance, these two gave the world an important survey of the
Tigris ; but at home such naval officers as Captain Ross Donnelly,
of H.M.S. *Pegasus*, were publishing through Laurie and Whittle
charts of north Scotland, Shetlands and Orkneys, " for the benefit
of the Royal Navy, &c., &c." Similarly the increase of trade with
North America caused the issue of new charts for the coast between
Halifax and Philadelphia.

It is true that in 1795 the British Government, having purchased
a collection of charts from the East India Company, thus founded
a basis of the Hydrographic Department of the Admiralty which
has since become world-famous for its accuracy and scope. But
when Nelson in 1801 was the driving force behind Parker ; when
the difficulties of navigating among the islands whereon Copenhagen stands had to be faced ; it was not by means of reliable
Admiralty charts that the fleet could be handled with confidence.
Nelson's freedom of manœuvre was hampered by lack of hydrographical knowledge, for the pilots were mostly those who had

been accustomed to trade between England and the Baltic, and necessarily were accustomed always to play for safety. Fairburn's plan is, however, interesting as showing how much the cartographers at that time knew.

Much more vivid is the aquatint (Plate 31, reproduced plain), showing the British fleet under way and the Danes lying to their anchors. This was published in 1801 after the picture by Nicholas Pocock, the engravers being Wells and Robert Pollard. The latter was born at Newcastle-on-Tyne in 1755; began life as a silversmith, and, after receiving some instruction from Richard Wilson, painted landscapes and seascapes. Finally he devoted himself to engraving in a peculiar mixed style of etching, line and aquatint. The print before us is one of a pair ; but Pollard in 1801 and 1807 did a series of four plates—also aquatints in colours—of this same Copenhagen event, yet depicted by Captain Cockburn, which are valued to-day at eighteen guineas. Pollard also did in colour " Nelson Advancing to meet the French Squadron at the Mouth of the Nile." This was copied from Pocock's picture and to-day changes hands at about £18. In the Copenhagen aquatint will be observed both the White and Blue Ensigns. Nelson had been appointed Vice-Admiral of the Blue on January 1, 1801. At Trafalgar we fought under the White Ensign only. The practice grew up of the fleet using one colour, and in the middle of the nineteenth century the red and blue were finally given up by the Royal Navy.

Pollard has been able to give us Pocock's picture of the British fleet running before the wind up the channel between Amak Island and the Middle Ground, with the Danish line of defence to port. And so well has the illustration been done that he would be a very dull person who could not imagine himself on board one of these vessels, with their big topsails and picturesque sterns. Hands

are seen aloft stowing the t'gallant sails whilst Nelson's division
is approaching to the attack. In this print the engraving was
actually done by Pollard, whilst Wells did the aquatinting. The
former was another craftsman who ended his days in poverty,
but he became an octogenarian.

It will have been noticed that painters and engravers were
offering not single-ship portraits but historic and spirited actions ;
and the obvious reason is that this was what the market desired.
It is, moreover, justified by the fact that (broadly speaking) there
had been no alterations in naval architecture since the time of the
Stuarts, and only comparatively minor alterations in the sails,
such as the abolition of the lateen mizzen in favour of canvas cut
in rectangular shape, and the full adoption of triangular headsails.
The decoration of hulls externally had gradually become less ornate,
steering wheels had been adopted in the Navy before 1747, and
decks were less lofty ; but, otherwise, the ships of the Anglo-Dutch
wars were not very different from those of the late Anglo-French.
Only after wars were being forgotten, and the clipper ship came
into prominence as a principal means of transport, were artists to
concentrate on individual ship portraiture, although this statement must be modified to include a number of stately well-armed
East Indiamen of the H.E. India Company. Still, often enough,
the background of some Oriental port is almost as important as the
Company's ship herself. This kind of vessel will be referred to
again presently.

But just as the old East Indiamen were the connecting links
between the seventeenth century and the golden age of sail, so
aquatints were the intermedium between line-engravings and
lithography. In its highest form the engraver draws direct on to
the copper some original work, rather than translating another
artist's ideas : but for the most part these ship prints are in fact

second-hand interpretations in terms of a separate skill. The love of colour is natural to the healthy-minded, and it is this which made aquatint colour-prints so popular a century ago. But to-day it is advisable to guard against the many " fake " colour-prints which have been produced by mechanical process on paper, stained to look old. A genuine aquatint after a good master such as Pocock is well worth a good price of eighteen or twenty pounds, for it is the nearest thing to a water-colour of the particular time.

Old historical ship prints to-day often need a great deal of search before they can be acquired, but it is well known that some of the best have been picked up for nominal prices. In 1804 there died an English engraver, who had been Lord Mayor of London in 1791, and his life is in contrast with so many craftsmen who died in poverty. John Boydell was a Shropshire lad, born in 1719, who came to London when he was about twenty-one and both by his craftsmanship and his print-trade did a great deal towards uplifting British engraving to the French standard, yet some of his marine subjects can still be obtained for three or four pounds. Boydell was responsible for the issue of more than four thousand plates, and among these the reader will discover those none too plentiful privateer items. Two of his French contemporaries, P. C. Canot (1710–1777) and N. B. F. Dequevauviller (1745–1807), also engraved in copper marine paintings of the period, such as fights between French ships and East Indiamen. Canot came over to England in 1740, and some of his best work was after Richard Paton's pictures. Dequevauviller was one of those artists whose work is marked by extreme delicacy and finish. Ships and atmosphere, figures and scenery, are all done most attractively.

Two engagements against the French, both depicted by T. Whitcombe, and both afterwards done by aquatint in colour, will be studied with genuine pleasure. For they are as interesting with regard to their subject as they are artistically. The first records the occasion of May 3, 1810, in the Bay of Naples, and this print was by J. Bailey. The second concerns H.M.S. *Amelia* and the French frigate *L'Aréthuse* during the night action of February 7, 1813, the engraving being by T. Sutherland. They were published in 1812 and 1817 respectively, the circumstances being as follows.

The Peace of Amiens had not been definitely concluded until 1802, but immediately afterwards it became apparent that there still remained a feverish uncertain suspense, and that the ambitions of Napoleon clashing with the attitude of England would culminate in another international crisis. This arrived with the renewal of war in 1804, which continued for the next ten years. We may pass over the intervening events and come to the first of May in the Mediterranean, 1810. The two British brigs *Spartan* and *Success* were cruising off the Italian coast when two French ships, a brig and a cutter, were discovered in the Bay of Naples. The two British vessels then immediately crowded on sail and pursued them almost to the Naples mole. Next morning the enemy were found lying at anchor still close under the land, so the British senior officer reasoned that the French would not come out whilst they knew the two brigs were in the offing. He even sent *Success* away more than fifteen miles to seaward of Capri, but *Spartan* was to appear off the mole of Naples at daylight in order to lure the enemy out.

At 4.30 a.m. on May 3, *Spartan* was standing into the Bay of Naples with a light morning air from the south-east. Half an hour later the French squadron was sighted coming out on the port tack, the force consisting of the frigate *Cérès*, the corvette *Fama*, the brig *Sparvière*, the cutter *Achille*, and seven cutter-rigged gunboats. So certain had the French been of overwhelming *Spartan* by all these craft and a superiority of ninety-five guns to thirty-eight, that four hundred Swiss troops had been sent in *Cérès* and *Fama* for the purpose of boarding the British ship. The decision was rash, for there are few more useless occasions than troops in a man-of-war. Not merely are they ineffective but they hamper the work of the sailors.

At 7 a.m. *Cérès*, *Fama*, and *Sparvière*, sailing in line ahead, tried to get on the windward side of *Spartan*, but the latter luffed and thwarted the enemy. Before eight o'clock the French Commodore was again steering with the wind abeam, and clewed up her courses, so *Spartan* did the same; and when within pistol shot of each other *Cérès* opened fire, but *Spartan* withheld hers until she was able to return a most destructive broadside. The carnage aboard *Cérès* was terrible, for the unhappy Swiss soldiers, who were drawn up in ranks ready to board, extended the whole length of the Frenchman's deck from cathead to taffrail. *Spartan* next engaged *Fama* and *Sparvière*.

Now in the meanwhile the French cutter and gunboats had been coming forth and *Spartan* now luffed to cut these off. At 8.13 a.m. she engaged them with her foremost starboard guns, then went about on the other tack, but whilst in stays deluged them with the whole of her port broadside, and with her starboard guns fired again at *Cérès*, *Fama*, and *Sparvière*. This was quite a smart piece of tactics, for *Spartan* had thus separated the fore-and-aft craft from the rest of the French squadron. By this time, also, *Cérès* (who was the Commodore's ship) decided that she had already seen enough fighting for one day, bore up and stood towards the batteries of Baia, so the British frigate went in pursuit of her.

Unluckily, just before nine the paltry air died away, so that *Spartan* was left with her head exposed to the raking fire of *Cérès* starboard broadside, whilst on *Spartan's* port bow were the corvette and brig, and astern were the cutter and gunboats coming up, propelled by means of their sweeps. Thus the British frigate was under a heavy concentrated fire, during which Captain J. Brenton, her commanding officer, was wounded as he stood on the capstan surveying the situation and conducting the fight. But just then came a light breeze which enabled the ships once more to move : that is to say, the enemy succeeded in gaining the protection of their Baia batteries, yet not before *Spartan* had raked frigate, corvette and brig. This was done with such success that she compelled the brig to haul down her colours and surrender at 10 a.m. At this moment it was the gallant dash of the French fore-and-aft cutter and gun- boats which came down and saved the crippled *Fama*, by towing her away ; but soon afterwards the true sea-breeze set in from the south-west, *Spartan* repaired her disabled rigging and went sailing away with her prize in triumph.

Now such a spectacular affair as this was just the kind of inspiration for an early nineteenth-century artist, and George Andrews, of " The Marine Print Warehouse," Charing Cross, got Bailey to make the aquatint after Whitcombe's charming painting, which was dedicated to Captain Brenton, officers and men. To the left of the print will be seen the three bigger French ships, with *Spartan* in the centre ; but many readers will find the flotilla of small craft to the right of especial interest. The cutter is seen carrying topsail and t'gallant : she is even hoisting a stuns'l to her topsail. Authorities differ as to whether there were seven or eight gunboats as well, but the artist has shown eight of them, the cutter being obviously the flotilla-leader. Thus, up to about a century ago, yacht-like craft were deemed not unworthy of taking part in naval warfare, as indeed they were to act again during the opera- tions of 1914–1918. When in a later chapter we examine the fore-and-afters more closely we must not forget this plucky little

French flotilla—the only enemy vessels which distinguished themselves that memorable morning in May.

The enthusiast will be able to obtain for his collection such aquatints in colours of this period as the following, among others, at the approximate prices indicated : the " Gallant Defence of *Arrow* and *Acheron*, on February 3–5, 1805, when in charge of a large convoy of 31 sail and attacked by two French frigates " (a pair of prints by J. Jeakes after F. Sartorius, rare, £38, published 1805) ; " Capture of the *Bergere*, April 17, 1806, by H.M. frigate *Sirius*, off the Tiber " (T. Sutherland, after T. Whitcombe, £1) ; " The *Northumberland* engaging a French squadron off L'Orient, May 22, 1812 " (by the same artists, £1) ; " Bombardment of Algiers, August 27, 1816, by Admiral Lord Exmouth " (by the same artists, published in 1816, £10 10s.) ; but for about a pound each various plates from such works as *Ralfe's Naval Chronicle* can be sometimes found, and from 1808 Rudolph Ackermann was issuing many books with aquatints. These items are, of course, not a complete list but are intended merely as suggestions for collectors beginning.

That unfortunate war between the United States and Britain, which began in 1812, it were best now to forget, but there are numerous aquatints and lithographs, especially of the famous incident in which *Chesapeake* and *Shannon* contended. There are aquatints and lithographs, too, of the Navarino battle in October, 1827. But an excellent aquatint in colour (here reproduced plain) showing the above Whitcombe-Sutherland combination will be found in the " Engagement between H.M.S *Amelia* and *L'Aréthuse*." This is another night action, and Whitcombe made his painting from sketches by J. C. Schetky. The scene is the west coast of Africa, the year 1813, and the drama opens at the end of January when the British 38-gun frigate *Amelia* (Captain the Hon. F. P.

Irby) was lying moored off Freetown, Sierra Leone, with a debilitated crew, for whose recovery she was about to sail towards England.

But intelligence came that two French frigates and a prize were at anchor off the Isle de Los to the northward. *Amelia* began to bend her sails and clear for action, got under way and made for that island in the hope of falling in with some British cruiser who might aid her against the enemy. For several merchant ships were daily expected at Sierra Leone, and thus the French frigates were in a position to attack this route of trade. On February 5 *Amelia* sighted Los, and on the following morning sighted also the Frenchmen at anchor, of whom one was the 48-gun frigate *L'Aréthuse* (Captain Bouvet), which now got under way. During the night she was not seen but was discovered on the morning of the 7th. Throughout the day a flukey wind delayed contact, but by the evening Captain Irby had succeeded in imposing his will to the extent that Bouvet had been drawn well away from the latter's consort. About 7 p.m. Irby, running under his three topsails with the wind on the starboard quarter, tried to cross the Frenchman's stern and thus rake her from aft, but Bouvet counteracted this by tacking to the south-west.

One must imagine now a moonlight night, with a very moderate wind and a lake-like sea. There was to be a fierce duel, with all the damage to wooden hulls and death to brave men. The details which James, with his meticulous care, gathered of this terrific fight are such as must inevitably fascinate every ship lover. Just before eight that evening *Amelia* had arrived within pistol-shot on the weather side. *Aréthuse* opened fire, but after three broadsides had been exchanged *Amelia* had the braces of her main topsail shot away, so that the sail was caught aback and she fell on the Frenchman. In so doing the latter's jib-boom carried away *Amelia's* jib and stay; the anchor-fluke of the enemy also fouled the Englishman's side.

This gave Bouvet's men in the tops and at the mastheads a fine opportunity to send down a heavy musketry fire as well as several hand-grenades, and parties were preparing to follow this up by boarding in the good old Tudor fashion. At this moment a man was seen on *Aréthuse's* spritsail yard (just below the bowsprit and clearly shown in the print) trying to climb across to *Amelia*. To the surprise of the Englishmen he cried out to them not to shoot, but immediately one of Irby's marines shot him so that he dropped down into the water like a dead bird. It was afterwards learnt that this was the man—a Hamburgher—who had formerly been one of *Amelia's* crew but had been captured by a French frigate out of a prize that *Amelia* had taken. He had been so anxious to regain his old ship that he had secreted himself aboard *Aréthuse*.

Presently Bouvet got his vessel clear, but *Amelia*, with her jib at present disabled, set her main t'gallant and middle staysails, and again tried to get across her enemy's bows so as to rake her. This was done, but at the second attempt she fell alongside so that the muzzles of the rival guns were almost touching. Thereupon followed an exhibition of brute force, of sword thrusts, of crashing explosions, until *Amelia's* quarterdeck had been cleared of both officers and men by the fire of the French musketry. It was the mutual concussion of guns which eventually forced the frigates apart, and they gradually drifted away until 11.20 p.m. when both sides, being out of range, ceased fire. The wonderful thing is that neither ship had lost a mast; but they were badly damaged, with rigging cut to pieces and hulls shattered: only the calm weather prevented further injuries. Irby had lost fifty-one and Bouvet thirty-one killed or mortally wounded. It was a long and bloody action while it lasted; each combatant withdrew through sheer exhaustion, and both had behaved with the greatest bravery. The rest of the night was spent in clearing the reddened decks of dead and wounded, securing the damaged masts, and in the morning *Amelia* made sail to Madeira and England ; for she had on board a considerable amount of gold-dust destined for English merchants, and her crew of invalids were at last to think again of home. Captain Bouvet stood in towards Isle de Los and presently sailed north to France.

Such was the incident which produced this print, and some of these frigate fights make up the most stirring of sea stories. This class of ship had during the eighteenth and early nineteenth centuries been passing through interesting phases. From the French shipbuilders much had been learnt, but the American war of 1812 had caused Britain to realize that the United States could build better frigates than the old country seemed to possess. There was something in the idea, but the notion was unduly pressed, so that big ships were cut down and converted at great expense. The advantages claimed were superiority in sailing, and pamphlets were written by naval officers advocating cutting down the smaller 74's. Some frigates were built of pitch-pine for lightness, with very thin and inadequate scantling, but the term " frigate " was not always strictly used. Its true meaning signified a vessel with a single-battery deck from stem to stern, yet it was applied to a ship which had two additional short decks upon which were mounted nearly as many guns as were carried on her whole deck.

Other officers were busy trying to improve the sail plans, which were still in great need of reform. Thus, Captain Sir Henry Heathcote put forward a suggestion for a more complete use of staysails and jib topsails, the aim being to set more canvas quickly yet to get them stowed snugly at the approach of a squall. It was from the Dutch that staysails had been brought into English ships, though we were a long time adopting this handy form of sail in a whole-hearted manner. Captain Heathcote was merely thinking a little ahead of his time and his method is well illustrated by the print on Plate 33, which is additionally interesting because it is one of the early lithographs. The design was drawn on stone by A. Aglio after A. Webb.

Lithography owes its invention to Aloys Senefelder (1771–1834), a German who was not an artist but a printer, who had previously been an unsuccessful actor. The basic idea is the antipathy of grease and water plus the readiness of certain stones to absorb grease and water equally. The stone is inked with a roller, but the pigment adheres only to those parts which have been covered with a specially greasy kind of chalk employed for making the design. The surface chalk is washed away by turpentine before the printing, but the grease is retained in the pores of the stone. The latter is quarried in Bavaria. Later on we shall observe that it is lithography which has preserved to us those wonderful ships of the clipper era, but we have still to see one more naval action which was reproduced by aquatint in colour. This is an Ackermann print by E. Duncan after W. Joy, and the subject-matter is one of those incidents off the West African coast.

In those waters sailed well-armed slave traders under the Spanish flag, and piratical craft with crews of lawless adventurers belonging to various nationalities, the chief area being the Bight of Benin. With their national love of freedom, the British Government backed by public opinion had, after the downfall of Napoleon and the settlement with America, sent a small naval squadron to stamp out the horrible trade that was being done by Spanish brigs and schooners. A midshipman, Mr. R. B. Crawford of H.M.S. *Esk*, had been put in charge of a prize named the *Neptuno*. He had with him only five men and one gun, when he was attacked in the Benin Bight by a Spanish pirate ship *Carolina*, carrying ninety men and two guns. In Duncan's print we are present during the middle of the engagement, which lasted for two strenuous hours, after which the pirate was compelled to haul off with the loss of about twenty men killed. The print was dedicated by Ackermann to Sir Charles Buller, C.B., Commodore of the ships and vessels on the West African station. The date of the incident was March 20, 1826, but the engraving was not published until ten years later.

We mentioned just now those stout little ships of two masts called brigs. These in one way and another have played no small part in naval history. Some of the world's greatest seamen, such as Cook the explorer, learned their profession aboard them, and the famous collier-brigs which used to carry coal from the Tyne to the Thames formed a fleet in which the sailor's art reached a marvellous excellence. The work of beating to windward through shoals and narrow waters, sometimes in company of several hundreds of such craft, and the competition to reach London first, made it essential that only efficient crews should be employed. During the eighteenth century such vessels were of about two hundred tons, but when in the nineteenth the cheap-built coffin ships with iron hulls and steam came into the trade, the coasting brig was doomed. She contended for a while but finally departed. In the Royal Navy, however, the brig continued till considerably later; in fact she was the last sailing ship to remain in that service, and some of us can still remember to have seen them under way twenty years ago.

Their final days saw this type employed as training ships, but in the 1830's they were still being built. Thus in 1836 was launched H.M.S. *Martin*, two years later Sir William Symonds had designed *Fantome* (726 tons), but in 1844 the Admiralty were building a series of brigs known as the " experimental squadron."

Of these one was *Mutine* (428 tons, 12 guns), but she was lost in 1848. Another was the *Flying Fish* from Symonds's design, built at Pembroke in 1843–1844, and the *Kingfisher* was constructed on the same lines in 1845. The *Espiègle* was launched at Chatham in 1844, but was sold in 1861. So advanced was scientific thought in 1846 that the Admiralty built in a private yard at Blackwall a 12-gun brig of iron, but so great was the prejudice in certain circles against the use of iron that she was never allowed to make her trials against the wooden brigs, and she was eventually sold out of the service.

Most fortunately H. J. Vernon was living at the time of the experimental brigs and in the lithograph on Plate 36 (which was done in colour) he has shown us four of them with great detail. Reading from left to right is the 16-gun *Cruizer*, then in the foreground comes the 12-gun *Flying Fish*, and to the right will be seen her two 12-gun sisters *Mutine* and *Daring*. Pretty little ships, and splendid schools for training boys to become sailors, one still hears handed down amusing stories of the life aboard these craft ; and there are those experts who believe that it would do no harm to have one or two of the brigs back for educational purposes even nowadays. This print can still be picked up for about £3 and is worth collecting.

Vernon was an artist who has left us one of the most illuminative illustrations concerning the British Navy under canvas. His lithograph entitled " The Channel Fleet bearing up and making sail down Channel," on May 13, 1846, commemorated for all time a sight that will never be witnessed again ; for here are seven great ships with their unwieldy but picturesque hulls coming along under white clouds and creating a perfect picture for any lover of the beautiful. There is not a naval officer afloat to-day who could manœuvre such a sail-driven squadron : there would not be one officer of the latter who would feel happy in a modern unsinkable steel battleship replete with every scientific ingenuity. What would the rough, hard-case, ignorant sailors of eighty years ago think of the naval seamen to-day with their education, their improved conditions aboard, their amusements and private wireless sets ?

Ships have altered so quickly in a couple of generations that every print or picture that has been in family care becomes suddenly of historic value. A few years ago the world spoke of the *Dreadnought* as the most wonderful shipbuilding effort conceived by the mind of man ; but to-day she is almost forgotten in the advance of progress, and before long her portrait will take on a special value. Now in Vernon's lithograph of the Channel Fleet the two biggest ships shown are the *Trafalgar* and *St. Vincent*, both of 120 guns. The lithograph in colour by T. Picken after W. Ranwell, published by Ackermann in 1842, gives us the actual launching of *Trafalgar* from Woolwich dockyard. This three-decker was considered so important that Queen Victoria went down to be present, and the royal standard is flying from one of the numerous craft assembled. The paddle steamers with their long, narrow smoke-stacks and old-fashioned bows remind one that early Victorian days are much further removed from our own period than can possibly be appreciated by mere numbers of years.

It helps us to realize how tenaciously the old wooden-wall convention lasted, if we study the print of the 131-gun *Marlborough*. This illustration is from a lithograph in colour by and after T. G. Dutton, who was working in London between 1845 and 1878, though one might select the period 1820–1860 as that when lithography was most practised in England. Dutton's prints are well worth collecting both for their æsthetic value as records

(Page 129)

THE EXPERIMENTAL BRIGS, ABOUT 1845.
Lithograph in colour by **H. J. VERNON.**

PLATE 36

(Page 130)   LAUNCH OF H.M.S. "TRAFALGAR." *Lithograph in colour by* T. PICKEN *after* W. RANWELL, *published* 1842.

(Page 130)   H.M.S. "MARLBOROUGH," ABOUT 1855. *Lithograph in colour, by and after* T. G. DUTTON.

PLATE 37

(Page 133) ARRIVING ABOARD ONE OF H.M. SHIPS AT SPITHEAD. *From a lithograph in colour,* 1831.

(Page 134) AFTER DINNER IN THE CAPTAIN'S CABIN. *From a lithograph in colour,* 1831.

PLATE 38

(Page 135)

UNIFORMS OF CAPTAIN AND LIEUTENANT, 1848. *One of* ACKERMANN'S *aquatints in colour.*

PLATE 39

(Page 135)

MIDSHIPMAN'S UNIFORM, 1828.
A rare lithograph in colour.

(Page 138)

EAST INDIAMAN CLOSEHAULED. *One of* ACKERMANN'S *aquatints of* 1801.

(Page 140)

CABINS AND SHIP'S STEWARD. *From a coloured line engraving after* BRYANT, 1805.

PLATE 40

An Interesting scene, on board an East-Indiaman, showing the Effects of a heavy Lurch, after dinner.

(Page 141)   **AT DINNER IN AN EAST INDIAMAN.** *From an etching in colour by* **GEORGE CRUIKSHANK, 1818.**

The Point of Honor.

(Page 141)   **FLOGGING A SEAMAN.** *From an etching in colour by* **GEORGE CRUIKSHANK, 1825.**

PLATE 41

(Page 140)

AN EAST INDIAMAN'S QUARTER DECK. *Aquatint in colour by and after* T. *and* W. DANIELL, 1810.

PLATE 42

(Page 144)   GRAVESEND IN 1828. *From* E. DUNCAN'S *aquatint in colour after* W. A. KNELL.

(Page 145)   BARQUE ENTERING WHITEHAVEN. *From* E. DUNCAN'S *aquatint in colour after* S. WALTERS, 1840.

PLATE 43

of bygone ships accurately presented and as an investment. Their price has of recent years considerably increased, and is likely to rise still further ; but a good Dutton lithograph in colours that can be picked up for £4 is well worth having.

The *Marlborough* was built in 1855 and should be compared with the *Trafalgar*. The latter had been built as a three-decker, but she was afterwards cut down to two decks and her armament reduced to 24 guns. She was given engines of only 500 horse-power, but the cost of building her as a sailing ship and converting her to a screw steamer was less than £165,000. She was finally placed out of commission in 1872. The *Marlborough*, on the other hand, whilst designed as a wooden line-of-battle ship and converted for auxiliary screw propulsion, was of greater tonnage and greater power. *Trafalgar's* displacement was 3,850 tons, but *Marlborough* displaced 6,050 tons and she could steam at over 11 knots with her 3,000 horse-power. She is to be regarded as the penultimate word in the last chapter of that long story of wooden battleships whose evolution we have seen expressed by the engravers. In her day *Marlborough* was regarded as the smartest vessel in the Royal Navy, but the year 1860 finally closed that period which goes back to the Tudors. Between 1855 and 1860 the British Admiralty in building a number of screw three-deckers certainly produced the finest heavy warships that could be made of wood. All the knowledge and experience of the Royal dockyards gained through three centuries were able to bring into being that 4,245-ton *Howe* with her two funnels, her propeller, but the old-fashioned sails and yards.

It seems extraordinary that half a century after Nelson's **death** a new man-of-war should be designed with seventeenth-century stern galleries, and that she should have her hull painted in the Nelsonian fashion with the old-time square ports, and her guns

OSP—K

distributed over three decks. But convention in the service died hard, First Lords of the Admiralty (such as Lord Melville) and designers (such as Sir William Symonds) had been opposed to the new-fangled ideas of steam. And then a different era came with the 9,000-ton iron-built and armoured *Warrior* of 1860, through which innovation all the modern navies take their development.

From the literature of the time we get to know something of the life aboard the wooden warships. Autobiographies are valuable, especially where they have been illustrated by contemporaries. There are also prints which from about the middle eighteenth century for another hundred years give caricatures of officers, men, and the service generally. Mr. Macpherson in his collection managed to include as many as 435 under this category alone. Other prints give us information concerning smuggling, fishing, and mere seascapes. There are sentimental prints of the time extolling Jack Tar ashore and afloat; in taverns revelling with his pals, making love to his admiring women; in country cottages yarning to his family; by the quayside paying a sorrowful farewell before going off for another long commission.

Literature and engravings did much to establish the convention that the sailor was an idle, dissolute fellow on land but a very gallant fellow on board. In the theatre he became a stock character as hero, with the Irishman as comic relief, and the tall dark villain as his rival. There was still a very distinct bulkhead between the landsman and the seafarer; the old prejudice against the sailor's profession continued till long after steam and luxury in liners had enticed people to voyage for pleasure and not unwillingly as a necessity. How distant seem those days when pilgrims crossed the mere Mediterranean in the discomfort of vermined galleys!

One of the best journals ever written by a pre-Victorian landsman concerning his experiences as a guest aboard one of H.M.

ships was by Robert Seymour, which Thomas M'Lean issued with lithographs in colour during 1831. These prints are full of humour and observation ; they take us into the low-roofed captain's after-cabin looking out over the stern, they enable us to dine in the ward-room or in the captain's cabin as the ship crosses the Bay of Biscay, while the port and the claret decanters go sweeping to leeward across the tablecloth. All the difficulties of a landsman trying to climb into his swinging bunk whilst the vessel gives a lurch and chairs come clattering around ; all the fun of the lower deck, with red-faced seamen dancing and fiddling ; all the unusual environment of ship-life so intrigued the artist that he has tried to make others see it in the same aspect. And now, nearly a hundred years afterwards, we are thankful that these lithographs have not been destroyed.

Two of these are here reproduced. One is intended to be the landsman arriving on board the two-decker at Spithead after he had been rowed from Portsmouth. A precarious ladder having been dropped over the side, he climbs his way up nervously.

" At twelve o'clock the same day," he remarks, " I was introduced into a new world ; on entering the after-cabin a floating drawing-room, with three French windows opening on a balcony. . . . Hearing the sound of a fife from below, and the measured tread of keeping time, I descended to the main deck to find the cause of the harmony. Nearly three hundred men were at the capstan, in the act of getting up the anchor. . . . Around the capstan stood the fifers nearly breathless, and petty officers as nearly so, encouraging the hard workers, and *gently* lecturing the lazy ones. We were delayed some time before heaving up the anchor—at which time the pushing, the fifing, and the scolding are at the extreme—waiting the tedious arrival of some smugglers, who were sentenced to three years' service in the Mediterranean . . . Twenty-four finer seamen never stepped a deck. . . . Among them was a gentleman . . . he was taken, I believe, in his own yacht, with *doubtful* goods on board ; and having refused to pay the fine allotted to him, he was sentenced to serve in the Mediterranean in the same manner as the rest of the prisoners."

Of the captain's dinner-party, here reproduced, Seymour remarked : " The dishes abounded in gravy that day, to the ruin of gold lace and smart uniforms," but one officer, " a *bon vivant*, rather than lose a glass of claret, that he had put to his lips at the commencement of a lurch, continued drinking while in the act of falling." The ward-room of this line-of-battle ship he describes as about thirty feet long, little more than half that wide, and on each side were the cabins. Cape de Roca (colloquially known to generations of seamen as the " Rock ") having been sighted before entering Lisbon, " we drank an additional bottle of champagne on the occasion, which did not sparkle more than our spirits." But a gale piped up, there was too much sea to cross the Tagus bar, so they had to put out into the Bay and get a good offing from de Roca. It was another week before the ship finally anchored off Lisbon.

By means of prints we are able to look at the uniforms worn by officers and men of the sailing-ship Navy. Aquatints and lithographs ; the engravings by J. A. Atkinson, who drew and etched his own aquatints ; L. Mansion, who worked with St. Eschauzier in the drawing on stone ; the prints published by Engelmann or Ackermann, or Miller, or Walker are valuable as affording positive information under this head, long before the camera and the half-tone process ended the career of engravers or lithographers. Atkinson, for instance, has left us an aquatint by which we know exactly how an admiral and a midshipman dressed in 1808. From Thomas Rowlandson (1756–1827), Dominic Serres, and George Cruikshank, hereinafter to be mentioned, we get etchings that throw light on this subject ; but the important fact to remember is that there was no uniformity in the officers' costumes until after the year 1747, when blue became the naval fundamental colour. Blue and gold uniform, white shirt, white waistcoat, white kneebreeches, and white stockings were the dress of an admiral at the beginning of the nineteenth century, and by the Engelmann lithograph (Plate 39) we can comprehend the uniform of a midshipman in the year 1828, when he was ranked as a first-class petty officer. This lithograph, by the way, belongs to a rare series of sixteen; but from a set of six aquatints in colour I have also selected the Ackermann print of 1848 giving in full dress a captain and lieutenant of the day.

In regard to the dress of seamen it may surprise the reader, accustomed to the modern bluejacket, when the statement is made that no established uniform was made until after the Russian war of 1855. Even as late as 1831, in Seymour's account mentioned above, whilst naval officers are shown in blue and gold and white, marines in red and white, the crew are dressed in multiform more akin to the present custom in some tramp steamers or coasting ketches. Some have a blue tunic and white trousers, others striped shirts or sweaters (with the ship's name across the chest after the manner of modern yacht-hands), whilst headgear ranged from red stocking caps to wide-brimmed straw hats and peaked caps. A seaman who served with Lord Howe on the " Glorious First of June " is shown in a contemporary mezzotint wearing striped trousers, waistcoat and scarf, and buttoned jacket, with fob below the waistcoat.

The fact is that these prints remind us how much that is revolutionary has happened in the appearance of ships and men during a century. Types come and go, new standards are set up and respected so quickly, that we forget some conventions are comparatively modern. It is just here that contemporary prints have such a preponderating importance. At the time when the plates or stones were made, the information seemed perfectly obvious ; but the essence of romance is distance, and about even those early and mid-Victorian prints there exists to-day an historic halo which some day will pertain to the cheap and unappreciated illustrations of our present ship life that we cast aside with the least appreciation.

But let us continue our investigation by reference now to those prints which carry us on to the climax of the sailing ships in the Mercantile Marine ; for they continued to use canvas and the old customs of wooden ships long after the Navy had become committed to steam and steel ; and we shall find that such illustrations, as have escaped destruction are well deserving of careful preservation and consideration.   Nor shall we approach these quaint subjects with anything but veneration : rather we shall admire the fact that there were pioneers who opened up new trade routes, built up trade routine, and kept going a grand tradition in spite of all the perils and discomforts of their period. The trend of modern attitude is to believe implicitly in that science which has annihilated maritime dangers. It is difficult to comprehend the trepidation with which our grandfathers voyaged to America or India ; but the fact is not the less historically true.

CHAPTER VIII

MERCHANT SHIP PRINTS

THE eighteenth-century ships of the Honourable East India Company well reflected the independence, the stateliness, the solidity and unruffled conservatism of that close corporation. The armament and fighting efficiency of these vessels differed but slightly from naval craft of similar size ; and indeed the Admiralty for many years of warfare relied on the invaluable help which the Company's marine was able to place at national disposal.

By the beginning of the nineteenth century practically the entire world's Oriental trade was in the English Company's hands, and the directors controlled a magnificent fleet of thirty or forty ships, ranging from about 600 to over 1,500 tons burthen. One thinks of these well-found vessels going out to India with troops, stores, officials ; but calling first at St. Helena, and sailing on from India to China. On the way out there was the risk, first, that one of H.M. ships would send a press-gang aboard and take out the pick of the crew for naval service. As likely as not the East Indiaman would be attacked the next day by a French privateer ; and whilst crossing the Indian Ocean she might have to fight her way against determined pirates lying in wait. Sometimes, too, a convoy of East Indiamen had to do battle with a squadron of French warships, and the Mercantile Marine senior officer had to show whether he was as good a tactician as the French admiral.

Ackermann in 1801 published an aquatint engraved by John

Hill (before the latter emigrated to America), which affords an excellent idea of " An Indiaman Close-Hauled." As the reader will observe, these vessels were cumbrous, heavy, and unhandy as compared with the later clippers, and many were lost by such accidents as getting ashore, by bad weather, and by fire, in addition to the losses during hostilities. As we read the memoirs of our ancestors, relating how they journeyed from London by road to join at Portsmouth some outward-bound East Indiaman, we can sympathize with the difficulties and uncertainties of travel that existed from the first. Whilst crossing Hounslow Heath it was always probable that robbers would waylay the coach, shoot the horses, and relieve the passengers of the money they were taking out to India. Some delay would usually occur at Spithead, but if the traveller had arrived safely on board he was in a state of trepidation as to what horrible occurrence would come next.

After beating down Channel and reaching the Bay of Biscay, encountering a gale and losing hands from aloft, the ship would get into fine weather and the passengers would begin to settle down to the strange life. Dancing took place, and there were occasions of exchanging visits when the wind was light and other vessels were in company. From St. Helena to Table Bay the Indiaman would carry right on, and then came the last long stretch across the Indian Ocean. But anything could still happen, for the ship might spring a leak—as quite often occurred—and the troops would have to help the tired crew at the pumps. Off Madagascar the pirates might be cruising about waiting; for this was a well-known base of lawless sea-rovers embracing all nationalities. Finally, if the patient passenger ever reached Bombay, he breathed a sigh of relief.

The ship herself had, however, begun her voyage at Blackwall and then dropped down to Gravesend, whence under the care of a pilot she had been brought to anchor in the Downs. Here some of the more daring London passengers would have joined, after being brought alongside by Deal boatmen for a fee of three to five guineas. Before long the passenger would be overcome by sea-sickness and retire to his swinging cot, or crawl behind the curtains into a coffin-like bunk. A rough steward in blue stocking-cap, with a muffler tightly fastened below an unshorn chin, would be in attendance ; but it might be some days before the passenger emerged from his cabin for meals.

Sometimes it took as long as three months from England to St. Helena, but much before that interval the passenger had been robbed by the soldiers aboard. These were the scum of the British Isles and were being sent out mostly to avoid prison. They came from the shore in a verminous condition, but immediately on deck were bathed in hot water and cleansed by scrubbing brushes, their clothes being then thrown over the side. For the offence of pilfering they were secured to the shrouds and severely flogged.

It was customary for passengers to bring on board with them their servants, their furniture, their wines. Dinner was at 2 p.m., candles had to be extinguished after supper by 9 p.m., and not a sound or a light must be made during the dark hours lest the ship should reveal her presence to privateers or pirates. General officers and Gentlemen in Council were allowed to bring with them as much as three tons of luggage, which included a table, a sofa (or couple of chairs), a washstand, and two chests of wine. This was always put aboard either at Gravesend or Portsmouth.

Now phases of all this life in the late eighteenth and early nineteenth centuries in H.E.I.C. ships have been illustrated not merely by the hack craftsmen, but by artists who actually travelled in these vessels. Thus William Daniell the painter (who was born in 1769) went, when he was fifteen, with his uncle Thomas Daniell, to India, and for the next ten years both were engaged in making

sketches for their great work on Oriental scenery. The two
Daniells afterwards drew and made an aquatint (see Plate 42) of
an East Indiaman's quarter deck, which was published in 1810.
The reader will find this reproduction an interesting complement
to Hill's illustration, for it gives one an every-day, intimate aspect
of the environment. The melodramatic bias is not absent, but
there are indicated some features of seafaring which all go to
make more perfect the pattern of maritime knowledge. Right
aft is seen the man at the wheel, ahead of him is a capstan, whilst
just forward of the mainmast are some of the ship's livestock, and
a couple of hands are lashing more securely the Indiaman's boats
stowed on deck. The bellying staysail, the heeling ship, the very
atmosphere suggested, all seem so real that we can almost listen
to the wind in the rigging. This is the kind of thing that makes
a picture sometimes far more dependable for information than what
we can ever discover in any ship-model.

William Daniell was no stranger to the sea, and his *Voyage
Round Great Britain*, published in eight volumes, consisting of more
than three hundred colour-plates, is well worth the twenty-five
guineas usually asked ; the separate plates are also obtainable
and should not be despised. But the coloured line-engraving
after Bryant, published in 1805, though not a work of beauty is
quite the sort of item for which the collector might keep an eye
lifting as he scrutinizes some old bookstall The æsthete would
pass over such a print, but he who tries to bring back pictorially
the past ships and their ways will gladly add this. On the left
is a two-berthed cabin aft, whilst on the right Bryant has given us
the ship's steward in blue. Those who travel thanklessly in luxury
liners to-day may well consider the accommodation in what were
unquestionably the finest merchant ships afloat about a hundred
and twenty years ago, yet very far from comfortable at that. It

was a time also when the master of the ship exercised far more authority over the passengers than ordinarily would be attempted by the commanding officer of a steamship to-day.

Thus every passenger was given a printed copy of the India-man's regulations, and the captain had to see that respect was maintained towards good manners or known usages and customs. It was a rule, for example, that when the captain retired from the table after dinner or supper, both passengers and officers must also leave. At the same time there was a good deal of heavy drink-ing done, and the conduct of some passengers became so scandalous that the Court of Directors bewailed the fact that " the good order and wholesome practices, formerly observed in the Company's ships, have been laid aside, and late hours and the consequent mischiefs introduced, by which the ship has been endangered and the decorum and propriety, which should be maintained, destroyed." There was, moreover, a quite considerable amount of smuggling done by homeward East Indiamen. Both the Company and the Board of Customs tried hard to stop it, but the high prices offered by receivers ashore were the more potent force.

Passengers were given a three-course dinner, but without fish. There was plenty of wine and beer carried, champagne being served twice a week. Ducks, fowls, sheep, pigs, a cow and calf were carried, in addition to " salt horse " and pickled tongues, so there was no lack of food. Theatricals and the usual ceremonies of crossing the line—and even bazaars—helped to break the monotony of the long voyages. But we can jump right into this life if we study the two accompanying illustrations by George Cruikshank, the famous caricaturist. These are from etchings in colour, for the eighteenth century had caused the development of a school of artists employing etching for caricature and satire ;

and in that connection one immediately thinks of Hogarth and Thomas Rowlandson.

George Cruikshank, whose period was from 1792 to 1878, was the son of Isaac Cruikshank, who, in turn, was a caricaturist contemporary with Rowlandson, and used to publish his prints through Laurie and Whittle, of whom we have already made mention. Luckily for us, George in very early life had a predilection for the sea, in spite of his mother's opposition, and in 1818 published " An Interesting scene, on board an East Indiaman, showing the Effects of a heavy Lurch, after dinner." The very environment we have just been discussing is here emphasized with biting sarcasm. In that low-roofed room, lit by the stern windows, the mid-day meal with its flowing liquor has been abruptly interrupted by the ship's violent motion, to the distress of the women passengers and annoyance of the men. Children are screaming, one of the crew is quietly imbibing during the confusion, whilst another exclaims to him cheerily : " My precious eyes, Tom ! Here's a smash ! " Then to the passengers : " Hold on, my hearties ! Hang on by your eyelids ! "

The black servant about to collapse with the steaming punch was one of those whom English gentlemen, after service in India, brought home with them and then discharged. By the terms of their obligation the Company were consequently put to great expense in carrying these natives back to their own country ; and the nuisance became so great that eventually the Directors refused to allow the coloured man on board except his master took a bond as security for the cost of sending the servant home. It will be noticed that the ship's guns are all ready to go into action at short notice, this being one of the standing regulations ; and temporary bulkheads could be dismantled throughout the ship immediately, so as to give facilities for movement fore and aft.

There can be little doubt that, apart altogether from the obvious satire, this etching gives a generally accurate picture. Cruikshank's brother Robert Isaac, who was two years older than George, began his career as midshipman in the Company's service and actually served in the *Perseverance*, but afterwards left the sea and made comic drawings in water-colour. This revival of etching included, of course, Turner's famous " Liber Studiorum," and even in our present second quarter of the twentieth century there are still a few artists who use this etching process to represent sailing ships.

In " The Point of Honour " Cruikshank had in mind a naval scene aboard one of H.M. ships, with the marines drawn up on the poop deck, the officers and crew assembled below, to witness the flogging of a seaman who has been secured by his wrists to a grating. A petty-officer is standing to the man's left with cat-o'-nine tails. Incidentally this print, which was published in 1825, bears out what was said in the previous chapter concerning the multiformity of sailors' costumes that still continued, and there are not two of the rough crowd dressed alike. That naval crews in those days were largely composed of " bad hats " and the worst lads of the village cannot be denied. Discipline had to be administered with a firmness that amounted to cruelty and barbarity—such as in that brutal custom of flogging a man round the fleet—for mutinies were only just below the surface.

But Cruikshank could not have been unaware that in the East India Company's ships the same harsh discipline was meted out to offenders. When a man was punished " with a dozen " for insolence or neglect of duty, the victim was first triced up by the thumbs and then the hefty bo'sun's mate with his cat flogged the wretched man's bare back. After this had been done a bucket of salt water washed away the blood, and the ship's routine could carry on. But there was plenty of trickiness among those in high places who should have known better, and it would have needed a caricaturist's power to indicate the abuses which went on over the sale of commands, or that extensive smuggling already mentioned. There is on record one case where a captain made in one outward and homeward voyage between London, China and London the goodly sum of £30,000!

Gravesend in those days saw the arrival and departure of these historic Indiamen, and we can still visualize the scene from Duncan's print which was published in 1828 after W. A. Knell. I have chosen this because it was at the date when at last the H.E.I.C. were about to lose their monopoly after so many generations of protected trading. Duncan made his engraving in colour aquatint, and there is something symbolical as we contemplate the young paddle steamer to the left now obtruding herself into a scene where the three-master and her sisters had always been queens of the sea. Already a new era, with unrestricted competition, was being announced : the old trade routes would soon be used by vessels that were entirely different from any which had voyaged before. In such views of seaports a collector can find both beauty and the story of marine development, and there is in conjunction with the maps a method of geographical study that for interest would be hard to beat.

Before 1820 the line-engraver almost always worked on copper or brass ; but after that date the steel plate was used by him just as steel was soon to be employed for building ships. This change among the artists was brought about because finer work could thus be done on a metal that was much more durable than the easily-worn copper surface. But aquatinting in colour was never more suitably employed than in handing on to posterity the pictures of ships and seaports belonging to the age when so many ancient marine matters were to undergo tremendous change. In the sphere of printing, the three-colour photographic process of the steel-ship age has been normally adopted for showing by illustrated books the hues of ships or any other subjects ; but that subtle quality and variety of tone achieved by the aquatint will continue to be associated with sailing ships of an unusually important period.

Another of Duncan's aquatints in colour is therefore here presented. This was after the picture by Samuel Walters of Liverpool, and is full of charm. The port is that of Whitehaven, Cumberland, and a barque is seen making for the entrance. Within is a fine fleet of square-rigged ships, for the collieries of the neighbourhood attracted a considerable amount of shipping. This print dates from 1840, and both artists have succeeded in giving a wonderful amount of character to the craft of that changing epoch. But in the aquatint by and after William Daniell, published in 1824, we have at last an effort to interpret the towering majesty of the sea and get away from the eighteenth-century conventional " drapery." The title is, " Off The Cape—A Man Overboard," and it was doubtless one of those incidents which had happened whilst Daniell with his uncle was on his way between India and England. A wave has struck the old East Indiaman, washing over the side a hen-coop and a man ; but a boat has been lowered and is being rowed towards him with all speed, whilst the passengers crowd the poop to wait and watch.

In this print you have all the suspense, the drama, the thrill which these early-nineteenth-century people loved to connect with the ships. There is an almost sensational striving after effect, but Daniell has really tried to break with insincerity and in its stead to give us the terror of the ocean as he saw it with his own eyes. The East Indiaman is under very short canvas, with only one of her topsails set, yet she has taken a heavy lurch to leeward, and just what is going to happen when she meets that next tremendous

wave Daniell cleverly leaves you to wonder. But the whole subject
is interrogatory. Will she be overwhelmed ? Will the lowered
boat be swamped ? Will the man escape from death as the fowls
are fluttering for their liberty within the wooden bars ? It is such
aquatinters as W. and T. Daniell, R. and D. Havell, and T.
Sutherland whose work should be regarded with gratitude. Some
of Daniell's plates out of his *Voyage round Great Britain* can be
picked up for about £1 each—that is to say, when found loose—and
they are well worth the price to one who collects ship prints. But
nowadays it may be taken as a working rule that aquatints
illustrating such subjects as naval, mercantile marine, coaching,
sporting or American views are expensive, owing to the laws of
supply and demand under the influence of present-day fashion.

W. J. Huggins, who was marine painter to William IV, made
a picture in 1832 of the Honourable East India Company's ship
Macqueen outward bound off the Start making a three-flag signal,
whilst inshore of her is another similar ship bound up Channel.
This delightful painting was reproduced during 1834 by aquatint
in colour, the engraver being C. Rosenberg, and we can well understand the reason for its appearance. For this was the very high-
water of the Company's glory, and the ebb was about to set in.
The Company had already lost their ancient exclusive right to
India, and now public opinion had demanded that the monopoly
with China should be broken down, so that any British shipowners
and merchants might be able to trade with the Orient. Thus the
Company's commercial charter came to an end in April, 1834, the
Directors became no longer traders but a council, which advised
and assisted in the control of political India. Twenty-three years
later came the Indian Mutiny, and on November 1, 1858, was
made the proclamation that the government had been transferred
from the East India Company to the British Sovereign. The

Company sold its fleet, sold its London headquarters, East India House, and thus an old tradition passed away ; but there were well-known shipping "free-traders" such as Joseph Somes (one of the founders of Lloyd's Register), and Wigram & Green, whose sailing ships from the Thames were to improve and modernize the East Indiamen beyond all thought. T. and W. Smith of Newcastle, as well as others, were also coming in with a less cumbrous type of " frigate " to take passengers and cargo between England, India, and China. But already in 1842 the P. & O. Company had begun to send steamers to India by the Cape of Good Hope.

Therefore this Huggins-Rosenberg print is symbolical of an all-important time ; and it is still obtainable. Interesting features are the wooden boat-davits on the quarter similar to those in use for the anchor ; the open square ports ; the hands busy in the tops ; the great depth of the single topsails, with smaller t'gallant and royal sails above ; but, lastly, the conservative retention of a high-steeved bowsprit with spritsail yard below. And since Huggins died in 1845, but had previously served afloat in the H.E.I.C., I think we can safely guarantee that every detail of *Macqueen*, in her departing glory, has been indicated with meticulous accuracy. It was the same C. Rosenberg who in 1833 produced a pair of aquatints after Huggins showing the Revenue cutter *Prince George*, and this pair now sells for at least twenty pounds.

In 1832 was published E. Duncan's aquatint in colour (here reproduced plain) of Huggins's picture entitled " Reefing Topsails," and we can thus imagine a section of life as it existed aboard such ships as *Macqueen*. Half a dozen hands in all sorts of costume— red, blue, and brown—are aloft making snug, singing and hauling, hanging on by their feet and fingers, whilst the man at the end of the yard, with his arm over the stuns'l boom, has just lost his hat. It is coming on to blow, and the " old man's " voice will presently curse them from the deck ; but as the ship rolls to and fro across the waters there is a cheery optimism along this topsail yard, and Huggins has managed to catch that breezy spirit.

Reefing topsails aboard these ships was, none the less, no fool's job, and required different management for almost every one of the four reefs which such ships could take in the sails. Four lines of reef-points will clearly be noticed in *Macqueen*'s topsails. When getting down a second reef, for example, it was advisable to clew up the t'gallants'ls if it was blowing at all fresh : otherwise the men might be swept away by the t'gallant sheets. But vessels could seldom endure t'gallants when a third reef in the topsail was necessary. Topsail yards were often carried away during reefing, from the neglect of hauling the topsail halyards taut before giving the word for the men to lie out along the yard. The result was that the whole weight of the men was suspended by the lifts, and thus both lives and yards were endangered. That was why the most experienced seamen were always very particular about this point before going aloft to reef. When getting near Cape Horn or the Cape of Good Hope, in the expectation of prolonged bad weather it was customary to send the t'gallant stuns'l booms down on deck, and to put life-lines on the topsail yards, about a foot off the yard, as a protection to the men.

The sea, however, was never intended to be safe, and never will be made danger-proof in spite of all the scientists and engineers. In those days piracy still continued in the Orient, the Occident and the Mediterranean. East Indiamen and tea-clippers becalmed in the China Sea were at times attacked by pirates in their junks, and during the first quarter of the nineteenth century the West Indian waters were not so well patrolled as to prevent piratical onslaughts on British merchant ships. The story of the West

Indiaman ship *Zephyr* and Aaron Smith, who was serving aboard her as first mate during 1822, is now part of history, yet a great romance too. I believe that this was the last trial for piracy which ever took place at the Old Bailey ; and it was whilst in the British Museum, looking through the pages of Dickens's *All the Year Round* for woodcuts contributed by Ford Madox Brown, that Mr. Ford Madox Ford came across a short account of Smith's trial. The subject gripped the novelist, and the result was that in collaboration with Joseph Conrad there was written the well-known novel, *Romance*.

In the Mediterranean the bombardment of Algiers by Lord Exmouth (previously mentioned as Sir Edward Pellew, but in 1814 made an admiral and a peer) had in 1816 cleared out a dangerous nest which had prospered for centuries ; yet for all that the Barbary pirates still continued, as they have to this day, and yachts returning from the Mediterranean, but becalmed off the north African coast, have within our own recollection been only just able to escape unpleasant attention. In their lateen-rigged, well-armed, three-masters the Barbarian corsairs, long after Exmouth's expedition, continued to roam about the sea for the well-filled merchantman, and the next illustration gives a view of Tetuan, within the Gibraltar Straits, showing a Barbary stronghold. In the foreground is the pirate lateener, who is being chased through the night by a French frigate. The latter has already opened fire, but the pirate is making an effort to reach safety. This aquatint in colour was published in 1831, having been engraved by J. Dower after the picture by Baugean and G. Webster.

The last days of sail were to be illustrated by the excellent lithographs which were produced until after mid-Victorian times, both in England and abroad. In France, whilst some artists such as Honoré Daumier (1808–1879) made their caricatures in this process, others reproduced landscape, architecture, sea-painting and so on. In 1801 there was born within Piedmont one who became a distinguished marine artist, whose work is seen in the next print. Felix Achille Saint-Aulaire did the shipping, V. Adam put in the figures, and C. Molle did the lithography. Saint-Aulaire had learnt his art under Ambroise Louis Garneray, mentioned in a previous chapter, and went on exhibiting in the Salon until the year 1838. He also did a certain amount of lithographic work himself. The illustration before us is rich with detail, and entitled " Ship taking a Pilot." An old-fashioned brig is seen with a three-masted lugger coming alongside, and the pilot is just being hauled aboard. The brig is running into harbour under top-sails, whilst hands are busy stowing. Saint-Aulaire has delighted in depicting just those points which would never have been stressed except by one who understood them as a sailor. I would select at chance the two stuns'l yards, or the hempen cable which has been protected from chafe at the hawse-pipe, or the men on the yard wrestling with the bunt of the sail, or the down-haul to one of the headsails, or the half-dozen other items which will strike a mariner's eye.

It was a United States brig named *Washington* which formed the subject of the picture painted and lithographed by A. Hoffy. The incident was when on September 8, 1846, this vessel (employed on survey work) was caught in a hurricane and capsized off Cape Hatteras. Hoffy did this illustration under the immediate super-vision of some surviving officers, and the print was afterwards published by him in Philadelphia. Cape Hatteras is that extremity of a low sandbank in North Carolina, notorious for its violent gales. When the sixteenth and seventeenth century English pioneers sailed out along that coast they were accustomed to find off this cape just the same bad weather ; and nineteenth-century

(Page 145)   OFF THE CAPE—A MAN OVERBOARD. *Aquatint by and after* WILLIAM DANIELL, 1824.

(Page 146)   HONOURABLE EAST INDIA COMPANY'S SHIP "MACQUEEN," 1832. *Aquatint in colour by* C. ROSENBERG *after* W. J. HUGGINS. *Published* 1834.

PLATE 44

(Page 147)   REEFING   TOPSAILS. *Aquatint   in   colour   by*
E. DUNCAN *after* W. J. HUGGINS, 1832.

(Page 149)   BARBARY PIRATE BEING CHASED BY FRENCH FRIGATE.
Aquatint in colour by J. DOWER, *published* 1831.

PLATE 45

(Page 150)   SHIP TAKING A PILOT. *Lithograph in colour after* F. A. SAINT-AULAIRE *by* V. ADAM *and* C. MOLLE, *about* 1830.

(Page 150)   LOSS OF U.S. BRIG "WASHINGTON" OFF CAPE HATTERAS. *Lithograph by* A. HOFFY, 1846.

PLATE 46

(Page 151)

TOWN OF SACRAMENTO. *French Lithograph by and after* N. LE BRETON, *about* 1850.

PLATE 47

(Page 152)   **BLACKWALL FRIGATE "BARHAM," BUILT 1846.**
Lithograph in colour by and after **T. G. DUTTON.**

(Page 152)   **BLACKWALL FRIGATE "TRAFALGAR," BUILT 1848.** *Litho-*
graph in colour by and after **T. G. DUTTON.**

PLATE 48

(Page 154)   CLIPPER SHIP "ETHEREAL," BUILT 1856. *Litho-graph in colour by* T. G. DUTTON.

(Page 154)   CLIPPER SHIP, "ESSEX," 1100 TONS. *Lithograph in colour by* T. G. DUTTON, 1862.

PLATE 49

(Page 155)

CLIPPER BARQUE "ALFRED HAWLEY," 420 TONS.
Lithograph in colour by T. G. DUTTON.

PLATE 50

DUTCH ADMIRALTY YACHT

DUTCH TRADING HOOKER

DUTCH SMACK

(Page 159)   DUTCH FORE-AND-AFTERS. *From the prints by* GERRIT GROENEWEGEN.

PLATE 51

logs tell the story of sailing vessels being overcome, yards and masts sent crashing over the side.

But attention is now directed to the lithograph which is the work of N. Le Breton after his own design, and it is a very rare as well as a very interesting print. This artist worked in London during the middle of the nineteenth century, though the print before us was actually done in Paris. We may well dismiss his lithographs as of small interest, always excepting his American views, his naval and marine subjects, which still have a steady demand among collectors. Thus his " Engagement between the *Kearsage* and the *Alabama*," lithographed in colour, fetches seventeen guineas. The " Town of Sacramento," here reproduced, is the earliest known view of that place and cannot be obtained for less than sixteen guineas.

We are back for a moment in those days which followed immediately on the California gold rush of 1849; when San Francisco began suddenly to rise from the importance of a small community; when wooden ships were being built feverishly to carry miners from eastern to western North America. To-day Sacramento, seventy-five miles up the river beyond San Francisco, is a considerable town; but here it is seen just a hamlet with a few trees cleared away to make a street, a few shacks erected as drug stores, the " Eldorado Exchange," " General Jackson's Hotel," the " Eagle Theatre," and even tents pitched by the newest arrivals.

Alongside the water-front float some of those ships which brought the speculators round the Horn, and there is also a paddle steamer named *Senator for San Francisco*, with one of the old-fashioned beam engines. We think of the old sea-chanteys which used to sing of this river, of the desperate passengers which the ships carried, and the wild crews who deserted to a man. There is a great deal in this print, and it is a really important document illustrative of California's early commerce ; but it is a lithograph which is bound to rise in value, so it should be obtained immediately the chance offers.

The period from about 1840 to 1870 will particularly concern collectors who specialize in sailing ships at the height of development ; for this was the time when, unrestricted by monopoly, unhampered by precedent, the shipbuilders and owners were putting on the ocean vessels that looked tall and handsome, but with their fine lines were even more remarkable still. The new order of things came with Richard Green's *Seringapatam*. She was of 818 tons, launched in the year Queen Victoria came to the throne, and became famous for quick and regular passages to the East. Thereafter followed a long list of other crack ships too numerous to indicate, though the next group of reproductions (after Dutton's splendid lithographs) show ship-portraiture at the very best. There was a time when Dutton's prints were not appreciated as they are to-day, and whenever the collector can find them at about £5 each they are unquestionably a good investment. For the sailing-ship age is gone, the airship era is upon us, and already the early prints of once despised steamships are becoming rare and valuable.

The *Barham*, which is shown flying at the main Green's house-flag, was built at Blackwall in 1846 for the East India route, and during nearly thirty years sailed backwards and forwards between England and the Orient. She was of 934 tons and could carry thirty-two guns, so easily she was comparable with a naval frigate. Two years later came another famous Blackwaller in which Green's flag will be seen even more distinctly. This was a vessel of 1,038 tons and still fought her way well into the 'seventies in spite of the all-conquering steamers. It is impossible to regard these

Thames frigates except with an emotion of pride tempered by regret that so fine a tradition has long since passed. Such vessels were the pick of the Mercantile Marine, they carried on a semi-naval routine, the officers were selected from good families whose elder sons had entered the Navy, there was great pride of ship, and altogether there existed a smartness and high standard of seamanship which to-day are absent from commercial vessels. Built of teak " well and faithfully," with the old-fashioned painted ports, they were a little heavy-sterned and massive afloat, but out of water their fine lines were at once recognized. They were not stinted in gear or personnel, and this *Trafalgar* carried, in addition to her captain, five mates, several midshipmen (*not* apprentices) who were usually invited to dine with the captain on Sundays or Thursdays when there was champagne on the table. Besides the crew of able seamen there were the bo'sun and his couple of mates, a sailmaker, cooper (who attended to the casks), and a fiddler who got busy at the capstan whilst the anchor was hove up to the old sailor tunes.

This *Trafalgar* must not be confused with Dunbar's ship of the same name, built at Sunderland in 1845 and of 715 tons. Duncan Dunbar owned a number of these newly introduced frigates, some of them being specially built out in India ; but we associate the famous Blackwallers particularly with the Green and Wigram families. The colour lithograph (Plate 52) enables one to picture the clipper ship *Sussex*, 1,100 tons, which was built by Money Wigram & Sons at Blackwall in 1852. She used to carry 70 passengers and 45 crew, but after many years of useful work was wrecked in 1871. If one turns back to contemporary records one finds that from about 1858 owners and captains had to lament the decay in both conduct and seamanship of the crews which now served these clippers, but the deterioration had been going on for the last ten or fifteen years : in fact, ever since steam definitely began to dominate the trade routes. The new type of man was usually found to be so inefficient that he could neither take the helm nor a cast of the lead. And as we admire Dutton's print we can sympathize with Captain William F. Fothergill, her commander, for his anxieties. But those ships which sailed to India and carried as passengers chiefly Army officers and their families, or Civil Servants, were stricter in discipline and more careful of routine than the Australian clippers with a generally democratic crowd of travellers going out to try their fortunes.

The *Ethereal* is a different clipper type, with a schooner-like bow and a prettier counter-like stern. The high steeved bowsprit has gone and the boat-davits are more in keeping with our modern usage, but there are many details awaiting the study of every enthusiast as he looks aloft and along. Every bit of cordage and rigging is in place, every sail drawing correctly from flying jib to cro'jack, and Dutton dared not have drawn the subject otherwise, for Captain Jarman, her skipper, or Messrs I. & W. B. Mills of Stockton-on-Tees, her owners, or Mr. John Pile of West Hartlepool, her builder, would never have tolerated the reproduction. This ship was built in 1856 and used to sail in the trade with China.

In the *Essex* lithograph Dutton has given us one of his very best efforts. This print was published in 1862, the ship having been launched at Blackwall only in the year previous. She was of 1,100 tons, built and owned by Money Wigram, Captain J. S. Atwood being in command ; and the reader will not omit to notice how the Blackwallers held on to the old-time fashion of painting the hull, long after the Nelson tradition had died out in North Country ports, where also (as exemplified in such ships as *Ethereal* and *Alfred Hawley*) the bowsprit and jib-boom made a much smaller angle with the sheer of the vessel. The artist must have seen

Essex just as he drew her, running before a hard wind under topsails, with hands aloft on the yards, out on the jib-boom end, and another party for'ard on deck ready to pass the warp to the tug which will shortly take her in tow up the Thames. Commander W. C. Crutchley, R.N.R., who died some years ago and once served in this beautiful clipper as an able-bodied seaman, had a great regard for Captain Atwood, as well as for her First Officer Gibbs. Four mates, in addition to midshipmen, bo'sun and the latter's two mates, and twenty-four able seamen made up a fine crew who worked the ship handsomely.

Gibbs was popular with the men, who thought none the less of him because they nicknamed him " Lady Jane." He had his own valet, he was not above dressing up in costume and singing at the ship's concert " The Lost Child " ; but the third mate was not loved. It was supposed to take four men to stow a t'gallantsail, and one of the methods by which a rattled crew could show their irritation towards an unpopular officer was not to sing when hauling on ropes at night-time, and thus prevent him knowing exactly what the men were doing. Silent men shortening sail were not strictly mutinous, but they were making the officer sufficiently anxious to reckon the score even. *Essex* was able to run up from Cape Horn to the Equator in sixteen days, but she had fine lines below water and enjoyed plenty of wind. There were at least three other well-known ships of this name. In the year 1816 the H.E.I. Company owned a vessel commanded by a Captain Nisbett which used to sail between the Thames and India ; in 1839 Wigram built at Blackwall an *Essex* of 776 tons ; and in 1863 Marshall at Sunderland launched an *Essex* of 1,200 tons.

In the lithograph of the clipper barque *Alfred Hawley*, 420 tons, there is so much similarity to *Ethereal* that one is not surprised to find she was built in the North Country—but this time by William

Pile of Sunderland. This comparatively small type may well end our long list of square-rigged ships as handed down to us by the masters of wood-engraving, line-engraving, etching, mezzotint, stipple, aquatint, and lithography. In each successive stage we have watched the artist and shipman learning and improving his task until the old East Indiaman, or the new clipper, through the medium of such men as Duncan and Dutton, seemed to reach perfection. If all the models and all the documents of these vessels were to-day destroyed, we should still be able by means of the prints to reconstruct the progress of naval architecture through the centuries wherein sea-travel, discovery, geographical study were going ahead collaterally with the reproduction of subjects in ink. A few years ago collectors forgot that some of the nineteenth-century journals and books contained lithographs which were deserving of preservation. The second-hand stalls and rubbish-heaps were raked through, with a result that to-day the sphere of search is more circumscribed. After a few more years, however, all kinds of ship-prints will be obtainable only by breaking up private collections ; and already the faded photographs of Victorian clippers are being sought with considerable eagerness. The lesson is obvious.

CHAPTER IX

PRINTS OF FORE-AND-AFT VESSELS

HITHERTO we have followed the engravers as they represented changing phases of the ocean-going ship with her one, two, or more square sails. Occasionally, as in Breydenbach's pilgrim galley, or in the Italian line-engraving of Genoa, we have met with the essentially Mediterranean lateen sail; and in de Bry's prints (such as that entitled " Benzon Reaches San Lucar de Barrameda ") we have noticed among the big ships a smaller and quite different type beginning to present itself. In the background also of that print representing the " Battle on the Zuyder Zee, October 11, 1573," this smaller craft is again quietly and unobtrusively indicated. Whilst Stefano della Bella showed us the seventeenth-century galleys of the Mediterranean, Nooms managed to etch in an occasional North European fore-and-after amongst his big square-riggers, and in Mulder's Amsterdam dockyard there was not omitted a Dutch yacht of the period.

The time has now come when it is necessary to see how the print-makers devoted themselves to the illustration of fore-and-afters exclusively. We desire, as a basis of our artistic study, to watch the chronological sequence of this second but most important kind of vessel. In other words, we would see with our eyes the evolution of the sloop, the cutter, the ketch, lugger, schooner, and others. Historically the square-sail, going back to the days of the ancient Egyptians on the Nile, is the oldest known rig in the world;

and the reason was that with the prevailing northerly wind these craft could sail against the river current, but, when returning down the Nile, they lowered mast and sail, so that by easy paddling they could be driven against the wind.

In the course of time—originating exactly when, or whence, we cannot say, though I hold the opinion that the lateen dates from the seventh century of the Christian era when Southern Europe came under the Arab's rule—the Mediterranean, preferring the triangular sail on a long yard, adopted what is very similar to that sail of the Arab dhow to this day. And it became known as " la voile latine," or the sail of the Latin peoples. Persistently this sail remained in the galleys, and when the ocean-going ship of the fifteenth century required a handy canvas-plan for her mizzen, she just added this lateen aft and became a three-master. Thus right down to the late eighteenth century a modified lateen mizzen still continued even in English line-of-battle ships. It is one more instance of maritime conservatism.

But in Northern Europe the lateen rig for smaller ships never held sway, although during the period when Spanish rule dominated Holland there were plenty of southern lateen galleys for a time in Dutch waters. Rather the germ of the northern idea is found in an open boat with a sprit lugsail to which was presently added a small triangular headsail. There is no evidence of this northern fore-and-aft rig before 1416, but it is in fact the modern cutter rig in embryo. De Bry's fishing-boat of 1594 is really very illuminative, for it was in the Low Countries that this rig had been inaugurated, and it was in those waters that he was accustomed to see the big ships and smaller fore-and-afters. He was engraving that which his own eyes saw, and his evidence is confirmed by other documents and by painting. Reference to this San Lucar print will prove that there was in established use a small cabin craft with what

(Page 153)

CLIPPER SHIP "SUSSEX," BUILT 1852. *Litho-graph in colour by* T. G. DUTTON.

PLATE 52

A View of His Majesty's Dock Yard at DEPTFORD, in the County of KENT, on the River Thames.

Vue du Chantier de Sa Majesté à DEPTFORD, dans le Comté de KENT, sur la Tamise.

(Page 160)

BOMB KETCH OFF DEPTFORD DOCKYARD.
Coloured line engraving published by CARINGTON BOWLES *after* JOHN CLEVELEY'S *painting in* 1772.

PLATE 53

is accurately termed a sloop rig. The sprit of the mainsail is supported by a tackle from the masthead, a vang from the peak leads aft to the steersman, and the sail is kept to the mast not by hoops but by lacing. The Zuyder Zee print has three such craft under way in 1573, but one also finds this rig somewhat shyly introduced in contemporary maps.

The Netherlands popularized this rig, developed it, modified it, improved it because it was essential for their inland waterways, especially the East and West Scheldts and the Maas, with all the waterborne traffic to Antwerp, Flushing, Rotterdam, Dordrecht, Gouda, and so on. The great wealth which came to Holland during the seventeenth century from her fisheries and the East Indies encouraged the building of many species, and not least of these the yacht for the use of the Navy, the East India Company officials, and for carrying distinguished personages from town to town. Of these there exist splendid illustrations by Van der Velde, by other great Dutch marine masters of the seventeenth century, as well as by the etcher Nooms. It was thus that by the presentation of the *Mary* from the Dutch to Charles II the yacht was first introduced into England, where it was to inaugurate a category of craft that should be used for such diverse purposes as pleasure, war, trade, smuggling, and revenue-protection.

And in the following century the engravers, the model-makers, as well as the painters, continued to represent these contemporary little vessels with such detail that we have all the required information to-day. We have before us three most interesting prints by Gerrit Groenewegen, the Dutch painter and etcher, who was born at Rotterdam in 1754. He had studied under Muys and earned fame for his pictures of ships and marine views generally until he died in 1826. His prints are rare, but these three are selected because they give so excellently the characteristics of the fore-

and-afters which sprang from that kind of craft illustrated by de Bry.

The Dutch Admiralty " jagt," or yacht, has discarded the sprit for her mainsail, but it still has a vang on each side from the peak and there is no boom along the foot. She has also added a jib ahead of the foresail. The leeboards, the gunports, the windows and decorated square stern are all in accordance with the practice of the seventeenth century. Secondly, consider the *Koopvaardy Hoeker*, which was a vessel used solely for trade. With the two squaresails on her mainmast, but in other respects fore-and-aft rigged, she was thus a compromise between the old and new. She was, in fact, a ketch ; and at the end of the seventeenth century North European navies had demanded a vessel of about 200 tons which would be suitable for bombarding defences and be able to stand the recoil of the mortars. England, France, and Holland all used them, and there was left a large triangular space forward of the mainmast so as to allow freedom for the mortar's fire. This type was known as a " galiote à bombe," or bomb-ketch. Gradually they became obsolete as warships, but with triangular headsails they were very popular in the Dutch mercantile marine trading across the North Sea to our East Coast ports.

Groenewegen's third example is called a " Smak Schip." She is likewise ketch-rigged, but her two squaresails are set only when running : she is a pure fore-and-after. In the eighteenth century a " smak schip," or " semaque," was characterized by her great beam ; hence she was known as the " wijd-schip." It will be noticed that she stows her mainsail by brailing—just as the above Admiralty " jagt " did and the modern Thames barge still does. But we are afforded an excellent opportunity of studying an English naval bomb-ketch if we look at the next colour illustration. This gives in the background His Majesty's dockyard at Deptford with several ships on the stocks, but in the foreground the bomb-ketch as she appeared in 1772, with the wide fore triangle, the square yards and quaint windowed stern, is more clearly portrayed. Incidentally, to the left may be noticed an English naval cutter, with her fore-and-aft rig but square topsail.

This print is from a coloured line-engraving which Carington Bowles of St. Paul's Churchyard published at the beginning of the year mentioned, after the painting by John Cleveley, the marine artist who was born in London about the year 1745. The latter spent the early years of his life in Deptford Dockyard, studied water-colour painting, and afterwards became a draughtsman in the Royal Navy. So keen was Cleveley on seafaring that in 1774 he went with an expedition of discovery to the Arctic regions, and with Sir Joseph Banks, President of the Royal Society, he visited Iceland. Cleveley died in 1786 and quite a lot of his drawings were engraved. His art can scarcely be called consummate, but certainly he had every opportunity for understanding the ships of his time, and he was just able to give us this contemporary bomb-ketch before the vessel finally was banished from the Navy. The little lugger to the right is worth bearing in mind for comparison with another print presently to be mentioned.

Very delightful are the two line-engravings which B. T. Pouncy made after John Kitchingman and published in the year 1783. Pouncy was brother-in-law of William Woollett, the draughtsman and engraver (1735–1785), who was made historical engraver to George III and copied such pictures as West's " Death of General Wolfe," and " Battle of La Hogue." From Woollett did Pouncy learn his art, and it will be realized from such plates as " Building of a Cutter " and " Chace of a Cutter," how excellent was his work. He used to exhibit at the Royal Academy from 1782–1789, and died at Lambeth ten years later.

We are to carry our minds back to a period when the King's Revenue cutters were engaged in an almost ceaseless campaign against those daring and desperate fellows who used to sail across from the Continent with cargoes of tea, tobacco, brandy, and other goods, which were smuggled ashore as opportunity permitted. These cutters were necessarily well armed and there were some fierce encounters, frequently attended by bloodshed. Still, the smugglers were very determined, could put up a good fight, and possessed some very fine craft. In this same year 1783, for instance, there was a notorious cutter named the *Swift* of Bridport, which was able to land about 2,000 casks of spirit as well as four or five tons of tea on each occasion that she came stealthily into Torbay. She was of 100 tons burthen, carried sixteen guns, and a crew of fifty; but the *Ranger*, another dangerous smuggler, was of 250 tons, carried nearly a hundred crew, and mounted twenty-two guns.

Therefore it was essential that the Revenue sloops or cutters should be well armed and well manned too. The service had become so large that in 1784 there were forty-four of these fore-and-afters and more than a thousand men employed, costing the Government just under £45,000 every year. All this activity gave no little encouragement to the builders of cutters. Seaworthiness, strength, and speed were required and demanded by both parties, so that it was not a rare occurrence to find a King's cutter and an intended smuggler being built side by side. Pouncy's first engraving is valuable as affording a view of a cutter nearing completion. There are gun-ports for a dozen guns, she is to have four shrouds on either side, in addition to backstays, she has a long straight keel for keeping a steady course when she pursues her enemy, and she still has that short square-tuck stern inherited from the Dutch. Altogether the under-water lines have been shown so clearly from this print that we can hand on to succeeding generations the exact appearance of a once-famous type.

In his second print Pouncy has sent such a craft to sea with a smart breeze to chase one of the smugglers, and already, as this King's ship goes smashing over the waves, she opens fire with her starboard bow gun. The details of the gear are most valuable for future historical reference, but we may just pause a moment to compare a slight difference in sail-plans. The chaser has set both a well-goared topsail and t'gallantsail above, whilst the pursued prefers to carry one large squaresail and one large topsail. But in addition to these great expanses of canvas it was customary to carry even stuns'ls, and a ring-tail (which was set abaft the leach of the mainsail). In this second print Pouncy has engraved sheets, blocks, dead-eyes and stays with most careful art. These are not rare prints, but for their beauty as well as their fidelity they are deserving of the collector's selection.

It was not every artist who could faithfully draw a ship : the numbers of the competent were proportionately as few as they are to-day. And it was for this reason that John Thomas Serres in 1805 published his *Liber Nauticus*, of which the first part was by himself and the second was by his father, giving a total of forty-one plates. In his preface the son remarks that

" many are the obstacles to the attainment of a proficiency in drawing Marine subjects, particularly as it is not only requisite that a person desirous of excelling in this Art should possess a knowledge of the construction of a Ship, or of what is denominated ' Naval Architecture ' together with the proportion of masts and yards, the width, depth & cut of the sails, &c., but he should likewise be acquainted with Seamanship.

" The second Part of this Work consists of Twenty-four Subjects, by Dominick Serres, Esq. late Marine Painter to His Majesty. They were made expressly for the instruction of a Nobleman," it goes on to state, " who, in testimony of the esteem which he had for the Artist, and the love which he entertaines for the Arts, conceived that to withold so valuable a work, from the Amateurs of Marine Drawing, would be a general loss. He has, therefore, liberally condescended to permit them to be engraved for Publication."

Now this two-part publication is an exceedingly rare book, and I have chosen a couple of the aquatints which were made by J. Clarke and J. Hamble after Dominick (or Dominique) Serres the father, the native of Gascony who had run away to sea and became a master mariner. The first will especially interest Solent yachtsmen, for the pleasure vessels of over a hundred and twenty years ago were strong and massive rather than light and fast. This craft is actually a coaster, but similar to a sloop yacht, and she is seen coming down Southampton Water past Calshot Castle. Technically she is not a cutter but a sloop, for the latter differed from the former by having a fixed, steeved bowsprit, a jibstay and smaller sails. It was even decided by a judge in a certain trial during 1795 that whereas a standing or running bowsprit was common to both sloop and cutter, the jib-sheet of the cutter was twice as large as that of a sloop and had no stay, and the tack of a cutter's jib was hooked to a traveller! But the learned judge evidently knew as little about seafaring as a sailor does about law. The essential difference was that the cutter was bigger than the sloop, with a straight, unsteeved bowsprit that could be run in, and the cutter did not set her jib on a stay as seen in Serres' aquatint. The square topsail was, as he shows, furled to the yard except when running before the wind.

Now this coaster was, with her stern windows, taffrail, and so on, just like many of the contemporary yachts. The Plague and Great Fire of London had almost killed the sport which Charles II so much enjoyed and Mr. Pepys tried to endure, but by 1720 it was in a state of revival, and in 1775 the Duke of Cumberland founded the famous Cumberland Fleet, out of which the Royal Thames Yacht Club was to grow. But if the first regatta in England was held during that year within sight of St. Paul's Cathedral, it must be realized that yachting in those days was still under the Dutch influence as to bluff craft and the semi-naval tactics employed. It was rather a dignified parade and display than a race; the latter was a later and conquering development.

Thus as late as 1793 the Cumberland Fleet issued to its members such signals as were to be obeyed in these sea-demonstrations. The Union Jack hoisted at the peak aboard the Commodore's yacht meant that the other yachts were to form line ahead. If the Union were at the masthead it signified line abreast; the Red Ensign at the masthead was an order to weigh anchor. And from one of that Cumberland Society's rules I have copied the following, which is so in keeping with the spirit of these old engravings :

" Amusement being the principle Business of this Society, the Commodore hopes every Captain will answer his Signals, as soon as the Situation of the Vessel he Commands will admit : he flatters himself the rather in this when he considers that the Spectators will Judge from thence, of the Excellence of the respective Vessels, the Propriety of the Management of each, and the good Disposition of the Whole."

But in our twentieth century, when the Bermudian rig has become dominant in yachts, it will be not without interest to study the aquatint here of Serres's " Bermudian Sloop." One of H.M. ships has adapted to naval purposes the local rig ; for whilst she is armed with guns, sets her jib sloop-fashion along a stay, and carries the usual English square topsail, yet she has the typical raking Bermudian mast, though the gaff is just about as long as it would have been in England.

By means of these old prints we can understand life in the Revenue Service in a way that is not otherwise possible. Captain Marryat's novels with their breezy stories of this life are a little careless as to historical accuracy, and the contemporary engravings are far more reliable, especially when the artists were ex-sailors. Now one of the popular rigs of that time was the three-masted lugger, which was very fast on a wind but not handy. When, however, there were available large crews such as in the Royal Navy, or among the smuggling fraternity, or among rich yachtsmen of the olden *régime*, a big lugger of two hundred tons with such fancy additions as topmasts, topsails, staysails, jib and flying jib, was a desirable craft. The brandy-runners found them very convenient with their crowd of ready-helpers, and there was many an exciting chase between lugger and King's cutter. The Government therefore copied this type both for the Revenue service and against the French. The essential feature was the lugger's speed, but she would carry ten, twelve, and even fourteen guns, being under the command of a lieutenant.

An " Armed Lugger Close Hauled, With All Sail Set " is here reproduced in colour, and gives a perfect idea of this extreme effort to attain speed. This is from a lithograph in J. Rogers's *Celebrated Sailing Vessels*, published in 1825, the drawings on stone having been done by himself after a painting by Rowney and Foster. The collector may be able occasionally to pick up an odd plate, but the book is now very seldom found complete. If by chance it should be discovered on some hidden shelf, it deserves a considerate treatment. E. W. Cooke's " Sixty-Five plates of Shipping and Craft drawn and etched," by himself, and published in 1829, is another useful, reliable collection by a man who spent a good deal of time afloat. Such a volume can still be obtained at a reasonable price from second-hand dealers, though some

(Page 161)   BUILDING OF A CUTTER. *Line engraving by*
B. T. POUNCY *after* J. KITCHINGMAN, 1783.

(Page 161)   CHACE OF A CUTTER. *Line engraving by* B. T. POUNCY
after J. KITCHINGMAN, 1783.

PLATE 54

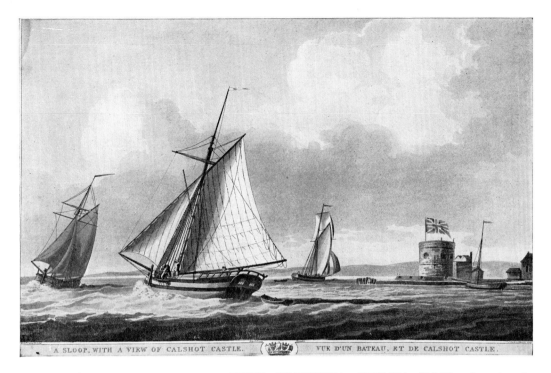

A SLOOP, WITH A VIEW OF CALSHOT CASTLE.   VUE D'UN BATEAU, ET DE CALSHOT CASTLE.

(Page 164)   EARLY NINETEENTH CENTURY SLOOP. *Aquatint by* J. CLARKE *and* J. HAMBLE *after* D. SERRES, 1805.

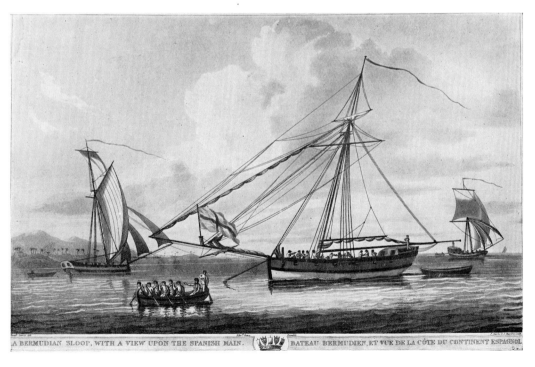

A BERMUDIAN SLOOP, WITH A VIEW UPON THE SPANISH MAIN.   BATEAU BERMUDIEN, ET VUE DE LA CÔTE DU CONTINENT ESPAGNOL.

(Page 165)   BERMUDIAN SLOOP, EARLY NINETEENTH CENTURY. *Aquatint by* J. CLARKE *and* J. HAMBLE *after* D. SERRES, 1805.

PLATE 55

(Page 167)   REVENUE CUTTER AND COBBLE LUGGER. *Aquatint by*
R. HAVELL AND SON *after* J. CARTWRIGHT, 1821.

(Page 168)   TRINITY HOUSE YACHT. *Anonymous print*
after W. J. HUGGINS, *about* 1830.

PLATE 56

(Page 168)

CUTTER ENTERING DOVER HARBOUR. *Aquatint in colour by* R. HAVELL *after* H. WHITFIELD, 1819.

PLATE 57

H.M. ARMED CUTTER "ACTIVE" SIGNALLING TO
ADMIRAL DUNCAN. *Aquatint by* E. DUNCAN *after*
W. J. HUGGINS, *published* 1830.

PLATE 58

(Page 172)

BALTIMORE CLIPPER SCHOONER. *Litho-graph by* N. CURRIER, *about* 1850.

(Page 176)

SAILING BARGE MATCH, JUNE 23, 1870. *One of* ACKERMANN'S *lithographs of* 1870

PLATE 59

(Page 173)   **CUTTER "BLUE BELL," 25 TONS, BUILT 1843.** *Lithograph in colour by* **T. G. DUTTON** *after* **C. TAYLOR.**

(Page 173)   **CUTTER "ENIGMA," 25 TONS, BUILT 1843.** *Lithograph by* **J. ROGERS.**

PLATE 60

(Page 173)   SCHOONER "FERNANDE" BEATING "MOSQUITO" AND
"CYNTHIA," 1849. *Aquatint by* YOUNG *after* N. M. CONDY.

(Page 174)   CUTTER "OSPREY," 59 TONS, BUILT 1859. *Lithograph by*
V. BROOKS *after* J. TAYLOR, *published in* 1863.

PLATE 61

(Page 166)

ARMED LUGGER CLOSE HAULED WITH ALL SAIL SET.
Lithograph in colour by J. ROGERS, 1825.

PLATE 62

(Page 168)

VIEW OF DUNDEE. *Aquatint in colour
after* I. CLARK, 1824.

PLATE 63

LEITH SMACK RUNNING UP SWIN, OCTOBER, 1838.
Lithograph in colour by J. C. SCHETKY.

PLATE 64

(Page 171)

AMERICAN TOPSAIL SCHOONER. *Lithograph in colour by* J. ROGERS, 1825.

PLATE 65

impressions are decidedly weak. But I am convinced that this series of smacks, schooners, barges, luggers, East and West India-men, warships and small boats, will soon become very scarce. It is one of the few occasions where an excellent drawing can be found of that almost obsolete boat the Yorkshire cobble.

Between the years 1800 and 1840 Robert and Daniel Havell were working in London as aquatint-engravers, and either individually or in collaboration produced a considerable number of plates, some of which were as illustrations to books whilst others were published separately. In addition to this they kept a large staff of good artists, and from 3, Chapel Street, just off Tottenham Court Road, issued such items as a set of Thames drawings after William Havell, a " View of Liverpool and Manchester Railway at Newton," and (in colour) the " Tower of London," " Bank of England," " Westminister Abbey," etc., which are nowadays worth two or three guineas. But the four aquatints after Pocock, published by Boydell in 1814, showing the " Battle between the English Frigate *Java* and the American Frigate *Constitution*," fought in December 1812, has so much historical attraction that it sells for £60. And here let it be noted that it is the historical prints which fetch especially high prices. Three years ago the sum of £112 was paid at a public auction for a pair of R. Havell's aquatints representing the " Storming of Fort Oswego " in 1814. Some idea of the rise in values may be appreciated when it is stated that a similar pair was sold some years previously for £8.

Our immediate concern is with the aquatint which Robert Havell and son issued in 1821 after the original drawing by J. Cartwright. This gives such a Revenue cutter as we have been discussing, with her straight bowsprit, her fourteen gunports, her squaresail yard lowered ; and she is about to weigh anchor as soon as the young flood makes. To the right of her is a three-masted

North Country fishing cobble rigged as a lugger. It is not a great work of art, but again it is one of those items which will become more and more valuable as the sailing craft become fewer. A rare item is the anonymous engraving of a Trinity House yacht after the painting by that W. J. Huggins whose other work we have already discussed. This is a most pleasing print, full of atmosphere and full of reliable instruction. The Trinity House flags, the carving at bow and stern, the faithful rendering of sails and rigging, the lowered squaresail and topsail yards, even the downhaul of the jib, are all indicated with an artistic appreciation and real loving understanding of ships. The date of this print is about 1830.

In the early nineteenth century there was a sudden enthusiasm for the harbours and ports of England by artists, engravers and printsellers. These views differ in quality, but some are by good artists and often contain illuminative flashes in regard to the period's ships. William Daniell's *Voyage round Great Britain*, containing more than three hundred plates, we have already mentioned; but two others may well be taken as examples of this new enthusiasm. The first is from an aquatint (Plate 57) by Robert Havell after Henry Whitfield and was published by Z. Warren in 1819. The scene is Dover harbour, with a cutter running in and a three-masted lugger reaching out. The twentieth-century tourist to France, who never remembers the time when the present vast breakwaters altered the bay into a national harbour for deep-draught ships, may find this print more than ordinarily intriguing. The second is also from an aquatint in colour after the painting by I. Clark, and was done for a book illustration in 1824. The subject is Dundee, with the famous whaling town in the distance, and a pilot cutter jilling about in the foreground under just enough sail to give her steerage way (Plate 63).

If, however, we would see the armed cutter in her most highly developed form as a Naval rather than a Revenue unit, we cannot do better than study the print of H.M. Armed Cutter *Active*, where she is seen close hauled with lowered topsail and triced mainsail firing a gun and making a signal to Admiral Duncan in Yarmouth Roads, giving intelligence that the Dutch Fleet were at sea. The inspiration of this picture is readily comprehended. Admiral Duncan was blockading the Dutch off the Texel until, at the beginning of October 1797, the exhaustion of his provisions and the damage to his ships by straining in the heavy autumnal weather caused him to sail back into Yarmouth for revictuals and a refit. He left behind to watch the movements of the enemy only three small vessels, viz., the frigate *Circe*, the armed cutter *Active*, and the lugger *Speculator*; but, naturally enough, when the Dutch discovered how slight was this force they sent out their fleet on October 7 and chased the three little craft away. Straight for Yarmouth the latter sailed in order to warn the admiral. Now the *Active* did outsail the other two and met a squadron under Captain Trollope whom Duncan was sending back to the Dutch coast. *Active* had so lured on the enemy that the Dutch admiral de Winter thought this must be the whole English squadron and turned back home, Trollope all the time keeping contact in the chase.

Active continued on her course and by October 9 approached Yarmouth Roads. The moment Duncan sighted the signal " Enemy at sea," the admiral hoisted in the *Venerable* a signal for a general chase. Before *Active* could come alongside, the whole fleet had weighed anchor and was running before the wind as shown in this picture. When the flagship came up with *Active*, Duncan hailed her commanding officer Captain J. Hamilton, and ordered him to pilot the fleet to the precise spot where the cutter had last seen the enemy. At daybreak of October 11 they all came in sight of the Texel and were joined by Captain Trollope. There followed the Battle of Camperdown, in which victory was gained by the British fleet.

The above picture of *Active* was painted by W. J. Huggins, engraved by E. Duncan in aquatint, published by Huggins not till the year 1830, and dedicated to Admiral Duncan, who had been rewarded with a peerage for the Camperdown victory. The cutter's good deed was indicative of the use which quite small vessels can perform to the Fleet ; and in that very same year 1797 it was the cutter *Viper* which was able to inform Jervis of the Spanish Fleet just before the Battle of St. Vincent. So also in its duty as a servant of the public the cutter in the early years of the nineteenth century was not less successful in the sphere of peace. There were the cutter-rigged packets which used to maintain connection between England and Calais, Great Yarmouth and Helvoetsluis in Holland, and also between London and Leith for Edinburgh.

The jolly lithograph in colour (Plate 64) by J. C. Schetky gives one of these Leith smacks running up the Swin Channel of the Thames estuary, whilst one of the collier brigs from the Tyne is beating to windward. It is one of those rare mellow days of early autumn, and the title is " A Leith Smack running up Swin with all sail set. Octr. 1838." It is a veritable white canvas cliff which is approaching, for she carried the following sails : mainsail, fore-and-aft topsail, square topsail, squaresail below the latter, and a jib forward. As to her " fancy stuff," she has set a watersail below the boom and another on a boom below the foot of the squaresail ; whilst on the port side she has a lower stuns'l and above it is a raffee or " angel's wing." A total of nine sails.

These Leith smacks were the Scotch expresses of the day. Full-bodied and bluff-bowed, with very long spars, a long straight keel nicely rounded at the forefoot, it used to be claimed that in 1819 and onwards this was " the most safe, convenient, and the most expeditious " of any similar service in Europe, and far superior to the brigs of 160–200 tons register which had only one small cabin. The origin of the passenger smack service was that there was already running from Berwick to London a number of smacks with cargoes of salmon ; so, finally, three companies from 1809 to 1814 were started to run from Leith to the Thames for travellers, with the result that the fleet numbered twenty-seven stout little cutters of 140 to 196 tons.

They each carried fourteen passengers in two cabins, one for men and one for women, with beds around each, but by 1819 small staterooms were being introduced. The crew consisted of master, mate, steward, and eleven men, and it was claimed for these smacks that they sailed nearer the wind and were faster than other vessels, and could do their eight knots or a day's run of 192 miles. On occasions the passage from London to Leith—reckoned as 430 miles—was done in forty-two hours. The cost of going from Edinburgh to London by the mail coach was £8 9s. for an inside ticket ; but what with subsistence, tips for the coachman and guard, a passenger could not escape for less than £12 ; whereas a cabin berth in a smack could be obtained for £3 13s. 6d., including provisions and beer.

But two more lithographs, of which the first is in colour, provide us with views of that rig which was so popular across the Atlantic in the nineteenth century, nor is yet by any means discarded. In origin it was descended from the influence of Dutch settlers of the late seventeenth century, and then by 1713 the first genuine American schooner with a triangular headsail was launched. During the nineteenth century Gloucester, especially, went on building these vessels, which reached such perfection that in 1851 the now historic schooner *America* came over into English waters and proved herself so successful that for a long time this rig became the most popular among yachtsmen able to afford big craft. The first print (Plate 65) is another lithograph by J. Rogers, and gives an American topsail schooner under reefed sails. The bow seems to have more overhang than we should have suspected, but from about 1800 to 1850 it was much more cut away than in corresponding British craft. The second (Plate 59) was done by N. Currier of Spruce, N.Y., and represents a Baltimore clipper of the mid-nineteenth century but rigged as a fore-and-aft schooner. In 1832 Baltimore had with *Ann McKim*, a vessel of 493 registered tons, brought out the first clipper vessel that was ever built, though it was the *Rainbow*, launched in New York during the year 1845, that set the real clipper fashion which was to revolutionize the stately East Indiamen into sea racehorses. Currier has given a dramatic touch by setting his clipper schooner hove-to in a gale of wind under trysail. His lithographs in colour fetch as low as a pound or two, but his print of the famous American clipper ship *Dreadnought* (after C. Parsons), which was launched in 1853, costs about £7 to-day, owing largely to her historical interest, for this was the ship of which the singing sailors used to chant. She was the last of the illustrious American clippers, and in 1853 crossed the Atlantic from New York to Liverpool in the remarkable time of fifteen days, but five years later reduced this time to thirteen days.

Happily the range of prints dealing with the evolution of yachts both in England and America is comprehensive and representative right down to the international *America* cup races of 1895. Although very little was engraved of the early days of yacht-racing on the Thames, yet it is still possible to obtain a few portraits of the vessels themselves. We must limit our selection to a dozen of these subjects which, by their outstanding interest, will give an outline of the material available. These characteristic types, with one exception, are all taken from lithographs. The influence of the contemporary Revenue cutter and smuggler was in the early stages most noticeable: in fact, the well-known yacht *Arrow*, which was built at Lymington in 1821, had been designed from the lines of a French smuggler which got wrecked. As we examine the cutter *Blue Bell* we immediately see the fashion just mentioned. This 25-ton cutter did a good deal of racing, from the year she was built in 1843, her competitors being such craft as Lord Alfred Paget's *Mystery*. *Blue Bell's* owner was Mr. Andrew Fountaine, to whom this print by T. G. Dutton (after C. Taylor) was dedicated.

She is further to be noted as one of the first yachts to be built of iron; but in that same year Mr. W. Read of Ipswich built for himself the 25-ton cutter *Enigma*, which is seen winning the Grand Challenge Gold Cup of the Royal Thames Yacht Club on June 8, 1843, the course being from Greenwich to below Gravesend and back and covered in four hours forty-five minutes. It was J. Rogers, again, who drew this on the stone, and the only non-lithographic print in this series is the aquatint by Young after N. M. Condy's picture, entitled "The *Fernande*, Royal Western Yacht Club, beating the *Mosquito* and *Cynthia* Cutters for the Queen's Vase, Plymouth, August 26, 1849." Condy was very fond of painting naval and other shipping in Plymouth Sound, and his little group of figures in the foreground is very characteristic.

In this print we observe an extraordinary family likeness to Currier's Baltimore Clipper as soon as the latter is compared with the *Fernande* schooner. The Blackwall frigates were necessarily partly responsible for this, but the Thames did not cease to modify also the cutters. *Mosquito*, 50-ton cutter, had been built in 1848 at the Thames Iron Works, and the first iron steamboat ever constructed had been tried on that river only twenty-six years previously.

It was, however, the *Great Britain* steamship which had a lot to do with the phase through which yachts were now passing. It will be recollected that this 3,618-ton vessel in 1846 ran ashore off the Irish coast, yet after a long and dangerous sojourn she was refloated and able to convince doubters of the merits of iron for building strong ships. *Mosquito* was designed with a straight stem, hollow bow, large displacement, well-raked sternpost and deep heel. She had a most successful career and finally became a pilot-cutter off Barrow-in-Furness.

The lithograph by V. Brooks after J. Taylor was published in 1863, and therein we see what an enormous thing was the old-fashioned topsail, as carried by the *Osprey*. This cutter was of 59 tons, she was built in 1859, in the same June won the £100 prize of the Royal Thames Yacht Club, in 1861 headed the winning list with prizes to the value of £410, and did very well in the year following. After the schooner *America* in 1851, during the race round the Isle of Wight, beat English yachts so handsomely, there ensued a veritable schooner craze. Such crack cutters as *Alarm* and *Arrow* were reconstructed as schooners, and new two-masters began to be laid down.

During this spasm, which was to last for nearly forty years, the two most important schooner yachts were unquestionably *Aline*, 216 tons, and *Egeria*, 153 tons. The former was built in 1860 by Camper & Nicholson for Mr. Charles Thellusson, and marked a new era by having masts that were not considerably raked aft but practically upright. Her sails were better cut, so that they were more lifting in character. Altogether *Aline* was a great success, and was the type on which the best schooners for the next five years were largely based. Dutton in 1867 made of her the accompanying beautiful tinted lithograph, which is worthy of a wonderfully attractive ship.

(Page 174) SCHOONER "ALINE," 216 TONS, BUILT 1860. *Lithograph, tinted, by* T. G. DUTTON *in* 1867.

(Page 175) SCHOONER "EGERIA" 153 TONS, BUILT 1865. *Lithograph in colour by* T. G. DUTTON, *published* 1876.

PLATE 66

(Page 175)

SCHOONER "LADY BUSK." *Lithograph by* T. G. DUTTON *after* HANS BUSK.

(Page 175)

YAWL "FLORINDA," BUILT 1873. *Lithograph by and after* T. G. DUTTON, *published* 1876.

PLATE 67

(Page 176)   AMERICAN SCHOONER "MOHAWK." *Lithograph published by* CURRIER & IVES, 1876.

(Page 176)   AMERICA CUP RACE OF 1876. *Chromolithograph after* F. S. COZZENS, *published* 1884.

PLATE 68

(Page 177)   "VOLUNTEER" BEATING "THISTLE," 1887. *Chromolithograph by* J. PRANG *after* J. G. TYLER, 1887.

(Page 178)   "DEFENDER" BEATING "VALKYRIE III," 1895. *Chromolithograph by* J. PRANG *after* J. G. TYLER, 1895.

PLATE 69

But in 1865 Wanhill of Poole built the schooner *Egeria*, which beat *Aline* in the Poole ship's maiden race, and became in fact the most successful British schooner that was ever launched.   Dutton's lithograph in colour published in 1876, showing her on a wind, is not artistically so pleasing as the last-mentioned, but it gives a good idea of the later clipper influence on these yachts. *Egeria* had a charmed and brilliant career, many vessels were built to beat her, but year after year she held her own, being particularly good in heavy weather.   She became the standard schooner yacht towards which other designers aimed, and it was all for the good of the sport : but by the late 'eighties schooner racing had finished its prosperity and the phase was over.

Of the schooner effect on contemporary cruising yachts there is a good example in Dutton's lithograph of the *Lady Busk*, owned and drawn by Captain Hans Busk. She may be compared with *Aline*, but she was not built for racing. *Lady Busk* was one of the early yachts to be fitted with auxiliary steam, her engines being of 80 horse-power, and she was certainly eye-pleasing with her graceful sheer. The lithograph of *Florinda* by and after Dutton is interesting as definitely illustrating for future historians another phase which has yet to die. This print, published in 1876, is worth collecting because *Florinda* was unbeatable during the first few years of her racing and was a serious menace to the schooner class. Hitherto the crack craft had been either of that rig or big cutters ; but *Florinda* was a yawl and she was spoken of as a " miracle " for speed. The result was that from now the yawls obtained a status and respect which had never previously been granted. Built by Camper & Nicholson in 1873, she not merely won a long list of prizes, but she was with her excellent accommodation a comfortable cruiser. Notice, please, that the old squaresail yard is carried and stowed at the mainmast just above the deck, after the manner in the Revenue cutters, when not running before the wind.

The " Eighth Annual Sailing Barge Match, June 23, 1870 " is from one of Ackermann's lithographs published in that same year, and is included for several reasons. Firstly, in these Thames barges we have the surviving influence, even at this second quarter of the twentieth century, of the Dutch rigs with their spritsails, vangs, and brails. The barge can thus claim a clear pedigree back to at least the early fifteenth century. Secondly, this Thames race was for many years one of the most delightful episodes which is comparable only with the annual races between the fishing smacks of Brixham. Unfortunately, after 1899 this oldtime barge race was allowed to lapse, but in 1927 it was decided to revive so excellent a custom, a cup being, as previously, presented by the Corporation of Lloyd's. Both the Medway and the bigger coasting barges have kept alive one of the finest schools of fore-and-aft seamanship and one of the most historic. How much longer it will survive steam engines and motors, who can tell ? This print shows the barge at her prime and is well worth adding to a collection.

Finally we have four lithographs from America. The first was published in 1876 by that firm Currier and Ives of which N. Currier has been already mentioned. The New York yacht *Mohawk* was the largest centre-board schooner ever built. She came out with an enormous sail area in 1875 and was the subject of much criticism. In the following year she was lying off Staten Island with her after canvas set, when there came a sudden squall which capsized her, drowning owner, his wife, and several others.

The chromolithograph after F. S. Cozzens, published in 1884, commemorates the *America* Cup race of 1876, when the schooner influence was still very strong. The Canadian schooner *Countess of Dufferin* was the challenger and the last of this rig so to do. She was not English but Canadian, being launched at Cobourg, Ontario, and then sailed round to New York. She measured 107 ft. long, with 24 ft. beam and 6½ ft. draught, a rakish bow and overhanging stern. Against her sailed the defender *Madeleine*, which had been built in 1868, but in 1876 was lengthened to 106 ft. with 24 ft. beam and 7 ft. 4 in. draught. She too had a centre-board, though this preference has never obtained in British yachts of any size. Unfortunately the Canadian had been built in a hurry and was not a success, so that, as seen in the print, *Madeleine* was able to beat her easily.

During the 'eighties in England the introduction of outside ballast instead of placing it below the floorboards had marked a fresh epoch, but that was not the only new idea. In 1887 that great naval architect G. L. Watson designed the British *Thistle*, which during that same year crossed the Atlantic to race for the America Cup against *Volunteer*, that had been constructed of steel by Burgess at Boston. The latter was much the faster ship, and, on the occasion of the second and final race held during the last day of September in the presence of a great fleet of steamers and yachts, *Thistle* was hopelessly beaten. That same year L. Prang made the accompanying chromolithograph after J. G. Tyler, and the sensational finish of the two clipper-bowed cutters has been set down for all time.

In the 'nineties came the last great modification to the racing yacht's hull. Both in England and America the clipper bow gave way to the spoon bow, and in the design every effort was made to reduce skin friction. When in 1895 *Valkyrie III* raced for the America Cup she found in *Defender* not merely the first *keel* yacht that had ever represented the United States in this contest, but one that had been built regardless of expense with a view to supreme lightness and speed, so far as a combination of bronze, steel and aluminium could provide in her deep-keeled hull. The result was as before, and *Defender* came romping home the victor. The event was given permanence in the chromolithograph by the same two artists, Tyler and Prang, which was published during that year.

Such, then, is our story of ship prints from the close of the fifteenth to the end of the nineteenth centuries. In yachting the recent adoption of the Bermudian rig ; in shipping the practically complete banishment of the square-rigger ; are the two great features which have marked the twentieth century. Otherwise these lithographs bring the narrative down to the present day. But in reproduction a complete change has occurred, the speed of life has been quickened, people can no longer wait months or even weeks for an engraving illustrating some worth-while event. Therefore the photographer has taken the place of the artist, immediacy is of greater import than permanence, a general idea to-day is of more value than a detailed study presented with excellent art later on. And yet to what fine excellence modern process work, in half tone and colour, can attain, let the reproduced prints in this volume bear witness.

INDEX

THE END